TESTING
TOP GUNS

UNITED STATES AIR FORCE AND NAVY TEST AND EVALUATION SQUADRONS

Edwards | Eglin | Nellis | Patuxent River | China Lake | Point Mugu

Jamie Hunter

MIDLAND
An imprint of
Ian Allan Publishing

The test squadrons of the United States Air Force and the United States Navy fly a rich diversity of aeroplanes and missions from these famous air bases to test and evaluate every new aeroplane or piece of new technology. They also dream up new ideas, try new ways of making things work, and work out how to best support the men and women on the front line.

The test bases and units detailed in this book hold a unique position due to their impressive missions, amazing technology and diversity of aircraft. The test community operates the old and the very new to complete its mission, making for a fascinating feast of aviation.

I have been fortunate enough to have spent time with all the incredible people at these amazing squadrons to record them in action. Flying in the F-14D over the Pacific with VX-30 'Bloodhounds' from Point Mugu, to the California Desert and Sierra Nevada in the F/A-18F Super Hornet with the 'Dust Devils' of VX-31 from China Lake, to the golden shores of the Gulf Coast in the F-16 with the 85th TES 'Skulls' from Eglin. Every moment of photographing, researching and compiling this book has been memorable.

So many people have given their precious time and unwavering assistance to make this book possible, and to them I am eternally grateful for the opportunity to take the images you see here. I would particularly like to thank Capt Bill 'Knuck' Chubb for his considerable support at China Lake and for writing the foreword. I would like to thank Lt Col Jerry 'Jive' Kerby for the honour of flying with the 82nd ATRS in the mighty F-4.

I would like to thank the following for their dedication and assistance in the compilation of this book:

USAF

Col William Coutts,
53rd Wing

Col Joseph Zeis,
46th Test Wing

Lt Col Anthony 'ET' Murphy

Lt Col Jerry 'Jive' Kerby

Lt Col Michael Vaccaro

Lt Col J Todd Hicks,
85th TES

Lt Col Sam 'Boomer' Shaneyfelt

Lt Col David 'Loogie' Lujan

Lt Col Jeff Weed

Lt Col Glenn Graham

Capt Doug 'Happy' Seymour

Capt Matt 'Goat' Allen

Capt Chris 'Bro' Heber

Capt Jason Medina,
SAFPAN

Capt Carlos Diaz

Capt Saje Park,
53rd Wing PA

Capt Daniel Dubois

Lt James Madeiros

TSgt Mary McHale

Sgt Cordner,
SAFPAN

Sgt Tonya Keebaugh

John Haire,
AFFTC PA

US NAVY

Capt Bill 'Knuck' Chubb

Capt Wade 'Torch' Knudson

Capt Bruce Fecht

Capt David Kennedy (Ret)

Cdr Timothy Morey

Cdr Tom Bourbeau

Cdr Rich Burr

Cdr John Fleming,
CHINFO

Lt Cdr Lance 'Pink' Floyd

Lt Cdr Mark 'Friday' Thomas

Lt Cdr Danny Hernandez
CHINFO

Lt Kent Jones

Lt Bryan Rex

Lt David Luckett,
CHINFO

Lt James Carroll

Lt David Neall

Bill Warlick

Doris Lance,
NAVAIR PA

James Darcy,
NAVAIR PA

John Romer,
NAVAIR PA

Adolf 'Mitch' Mitchell

Vance Vasquez

Mick Roth

John Milliman

I would also like to thank: Eric Hehs from Lockheed Martin's *Code One* magazine, Katsuhiko Tokunaga, Ted Carlson, Richard Cooper, Richard Collens, Paul Newman, Bill and Wesley Turner, Chris Pocock and Kevin Jackson.

The author's images were taken using Canon SLR EOS-1 digital and EOS-3 film cameras, with Fuji Provia 100F film.

USAF and US Navy imagery used in illustration without endorsement expressed or implied.

Jamie Hunter
Surrey, May 2006

Testing Top Guns © 2006 Jamie Hunter

ISBN (10) 1 85780 232 2
ISBN (13) 1 85780 232 0

Published by Midland Publishing
4 Watling Drive, Hinckley, LE10 3EY, England
Tel: 01455 254 490   Fax: 01455 254 495
E-mail: midlandbooks@compuserve.com

Midland Publishing is an imprint of
Ian Allan Publishing Ltd

Worldwide distribution (except North America):
Midland Counties Publications
4 Watling Drive, Hinckley, LE10 3EY, England
Telephone: 01455 254 450   Fax: 01455 233 737
E-mail: midlandbooks@compuserve.com
www.midlandcountiessuperstore.com

North American trade distribution:
Specialty Press Publishers & Wholesalers Inc.
39966 Grand Avenue, North Branch, MN 55056
Tel: 651 277 1400   Fax: 651 277 1203
Toll free telephone: 800 895 4585
www.specialtypress.com

Graphic Design © 2006 Philip Hempell

Printed in England by Ian Allan Printing Ltd
Riverdene Business Park, Molesey Road,
Hersham, Surrey, KT12 4RG

Visit the Ian Allan Publishing website at:
www.ianallanpublishing.com

Front cover, main: **An F-16B of the 40th FLTS from Eglin breaks for the camera.** *Jamie Hunter/AVIACOM*

Front cover, insets: Jamie Hunter/AVIACOM (two)
Katsuhiko Tokunaga (one)

Title page: Jamie Hunter/AVIACOM

Back cover: Jamie Hunter/AVIACOM

Foreword

By Captain W M Chubb, US Navy

'The Lake' has been a magical place for me since I flew in the surrounding airspace as an operational tester in the early 1990s. The ground sites on the ranges at China Lake and throughout the high desert complex add to the fascination of life in the southeastern Sierras. While I commanded the 'Dust Devils' of Air Test and Evaluation Squadron Three One in 2004/5, I had the pleasure of hosting Jamie Hunter as he was preparing this book. In his book he captures the magic of the soul of China Lake in words and images. He depicts the realities of testing cutting-edge weapons systems at a remote desert location.

His narration of the testing by the 'Dust Devils' of VX-31 for military aircraft aficionados goes beyond the roar of engines and smell of burnt fuel and cordite. This book reflects that reality; his readers gain a deeper awareness of the testers' sense of mission and purpose as they practice their craft in this fabulous complex of military airspace land ranges situated in the mountains of the Sierra Nevada Mountains and Mojave Desert of California.

Author Jamie Hunter is one of the most respected aviation photojournalists on the planet, his reputation for competence, impartiality, and friendly cooperation appears to go well beyond his native United Kingdom. It is a great honor to be asked to write a foreword to this tremendous documentary. I found the highlight of the book to be the chapters involving weapons testing. His enlightening analysis of the tester's mission is illustrated over and over again and he successfully shows how test pilots from all branches of the military have risen to meet the needs of their country.

Left: **Pulling hard round into the circuit pattern at China Lake as the afternoon autumnal light turns golden, a three-ship of VX-31 Hornets runs in for the break to land.** *Jamie Hunter/AVIACOM*

Below: **Capt Bill Chubb seen during his tenure as Commander of VX-31 'Dust Devils' at China Lake.** *Jamie Hunter/AVIACOM*

Introduction
Testing Today

Edwards | Eglin | Nellis | Patuxent River | China Lake | Point Mugu

'Leveling off at 42,000ft, I had thirty percent of my fuel, so I turned on rocket chamber three and immediately reached .96 Mach. I noticed that the faster I got, the smoother the ride. Suddenly the Mach needle began to fluctuate. It went up to .965 Mach – then tipped right off the scale...we were flying supersonic. And it was as smooth as a baby's bottom; Grandma could be sitting up there sipping lemonade'.

General Charles 'Chuck' Yeager

Roll with it – a USAF test F-16B flown by a test pilot from the 40th FLTS at Eglin demonstrates the incredible agility of today's fast jets. *Jamie Hunter/AVIACOM*

The US military is constantly testing and evaluating some of the most advanced aviation systems in the world for its front line. The USAF and US Navy have a host of squadrons devoted to these tasks dotted around some of the most interesting regions of the US. At the controls, some of the most gifted men and women flyers on the planet. On the ground, the most dedicated support personnel ensuring safe and effective testing. These squadrons boast some of the most diverse roles and most exciting flying in the world and allow a broad overview of the current status of all aircraft in the particular inventories. The squadrons boast some unique aircraft and rich histories, with stations such as Edwards and China Lake being the home to supersonic flight and cradle for nearly all of the current weapons systems in use. *Testing Top Guns* takes you into the cockpits and behind the scenes of these rarely seen squadrons.

The USAF test bases at Edwards and Eglin fly a host of interesting aircraft types and test them to the limit. At Nellis, the unique attributes of the ranges here are pivotal to evaluating and developing new operational doctrines. The US Navy test bases at Patuxent River, China Lake and Point Mugu do very much the same. Testing new weapons, introducing new capabilities, and honing current and future systems. These bases are steeped in history, none more so than Edwards. Although not designed as a history book, this work cannot be complete without a brief look at the origins of flight testing, and some of the incredible aeroplanes and test pilots that have shaped aviation history.

The test teams of today are following in the footsteps of yesterday's pioneers of aviation. Every mission is valued and every test point needs to be achieved safely and efficiently to meet operational requirements. The way this is achieved is constantly evolving to best meet requirements. It makes for an exciting and exhilarating ride with America's 'Testing Top Guns'.

Right: **Going ballistic! With full reheat engaged, a 40th Flight Test Squadron Lockheed Martin F-16 Fighting Falcon pilot races for the heavens from Eglin AFB.** *Jamie Hunter/AVIACOM*

Below: **Testing involves taking the latest equipment and pushing to the limit. Look no further than the Lockheed Martin F-22A Raptor for the latest and greatest. G-soaked aerial engagements above test ranges have proved the potential, written the tactics, and established the Raptor as the benchmark for the future.** *Jamie Hunter/AVIACOM*

Bottom: **Flight testing isn't just about new aircraft, It is also about taking existing hardware and making it better. Upgrades are more important now than ever before. Aircraft like this Boeing F/A-18C Hornet of VX-9 'Vampires' are kept busy evaluating new equipment for fleet squadrons.** *Jamie Hunter/AVIACOM*

Right: **A trio of Lockheed Martin F-16CJs of the 85th Test and Evaluation Squadron from Eglin AFB on the Gulf Coast of Florida. These jets are fitted with the latest technology. Incredible capabilities such as receiving real-time target images in the cockpit, identifying threat systems from long range and helmet sights are normal daily practice here.** *Jamie Hunter/AVIACOM*

Bottom left: **Test pilots are a special breed. The ability to work with a system, analyse it, work with it, develop it, takes skill and training. The USAF and US Navy can call upon some of the finest in the world.** *Jamie Hunter/AVIACOM*

Bottom right: **At sea aboard USS *Theodore Roosevelt* (CVN-71), a Boeing F/A-18E Super Hornet of Air Test and Evaluation Squadron Twenty Three (VX-23) 'Salty Dogs' from NAS Patuxent River in Maryland prepares to launch from one of the carrier's four steam catapults during flightdeck certification for the Super Hornet.** *US Navy/James Foehl*

Above: **Nicely illustrating the diversity of some of these test units, a quartet of VX-31 'Dust Devils' aircraft from China Lake led by unit commander Capt Bill Chubb in the Super Hornet. Holding a tight echelon left are Cdr Tim Morey in an immaculate F/A-18E, Cdr Rick Botham in an F/A-18A and a TAV-8B Harrier flown by Marine Corps test pilot Lt Col James 'Hawk' Hawkins.**
Jamie Hunter/AVIACOM

Below: **Heading into the blue above Edwards AFB, an early F-22A Raptor mission to push the flight handling of the type to see exactly what it can do.** *USAF/AFFTC*

Above: **At NAWS China Lake, in California's Mojave Desert, a test pilot from VX-31 'Dust Devils' heads out to his F/A-18F Super Hornet for a trials mission to evaluate a new reconnaissance pod.**
Jamie Hunter/AVIACOM

Above: **Engine start – Cdr Rich Burr of VX-30 'Bloodhounds' at NBVC Point Mugu signals the start-up for his F/A-18A Hornet prior to a 2v1 combat training mission over the Pacific Missile Test Ranges of southern California.** *Jamie Hunter/AVIACOM*

Top: **Lt Col J Todd Hicks in the Lockheed Martin Block 50 F-16CJ basking in the golden afternoon sunlight near Eglin AFB.** *Jamie Hunter/AVIACOM*

Right: **First look, first kill. The awesome Joint Helmet-Mounted Cueing System (JHMCS) worn here by Lt Col David Lujan in 'his' F-16D.** *Jamie Hunter/AVIACOM*

Above: **It's not just about fast jets, this NP-3D of VX-30 at Point Mugu provides vital range control for the many test missions carried out over the Pacific ranges near the base.**
Jamie Hunter/AVIACOM

Left: **Testing can still involve the weird and the wonderful. New programmes inevitably encounter development issues and setbacks. None more so than the Bell/Boeing V-22 Osprey programme that tragically suffered two fatal crashes in 2000 during testing. Thanks to the hard work and dedication of its test team, the Osprey has come through its troubles and has earned itself respect as a highly capable platform for the future.** *US Navy*

Below: **Safe landings.** *Jamie Hunter/AVIACOM*

Chapter One

Edwards AFB

Home of 'The Right Stuff'

In military flight testing there are few places that hold the reputation and the mystique of Edwards AFB, in California. Edwards has earned itself a unique reputation as the home of United States Air Force flight testing, a place where pilots push the barriers, explore the limits and fly to the extremes. This massive air base is part of Air Force Material Command (AFMC) and nestles on the edge of the Rogers Dry Lake bed in the arid, dusty Mojave Desert. For decades the remote desert canyons near here have echoed with sonic booms and the skies have been pierced by the sound of jet noise as the USAF Flight Test Center plies its trade to fly faster, higher and further.

Today, the shimmering flightlines at Edwards offer a less diverse but still impressive feast of aviation types and operations are still hectic, but sadly gone are the days of constant operations by the weird and wonderful. That said, the main aim here remains the same – test. The USAF mirrors other military air arms around the world, streamlining to be a smaller, more efficient force. Faster, higher and further has become cheaper, quicker and more efficient.

The history at Edwards is palpable. This base is steeped in history, and names such as Yeager, Crossfield and Knight all pushed the limits of flight testing here and are just some of those who have made history at Edwards.

The base itself actually traces its routes back to 1933 when it was established as March Field Bombing and Gunnery Range, a remote facility on the edge of Muroc Dry Lake. It wasn't long before strange shapes in the sky became the norm here as the remote location attracted a host of incredible new projects. In 1940 a pilot called Vance Breese got airborne from nearby Rogers Dry Lake in his N-1M flying wing, the very first record of flight testing here and the very first step towards the creation of the Air Force Flight Test Center (AFFTC). Breese worked for Jack Northrop and this was his new company's first project, marking the start of a succession of new flying machines from Northrop. This early flying wing was actually designed as a one-third scale model of a large flying wing bomber, the mighty XB-35, which was to fly later in June 1946.

September 1942 marked another era in the history of the base, when a dusty, anonymous freight train rumbled into the sleepy

Banking majestically above Joshua trees at Edwards AFB, one of the two Boeing XB-47 Stratojet prototypes with distinctive smoke trails from its six Ge J35-GE-7 turbojets in this evocative 1950s photo. *AFFTC*

Muroc siding. Inside the freight car was one of the most significant aircraft in the history of flight testing, America's first jet aircraft. The arrival of the top secret Bell XP-59A led to a portion of the lakebed being assigned for the exclusive use of Air Materiel Command, with a portable hangar and barracks hurriedly being erected. The most interesting arrival for this top-secret project was arguably the engines for the new aircraft. General Electric engineers were worried about the long train journey for the new technology and so the decision was made to keep the engines running over during the entire secretive delivery trip to prevent damage. On 2 October 1942

Left: **The arrival of America's first jet aircraft, the super-secret Bell XP-49A Airacomet, heralded the start of flight testing at Edwards when it arrived here in 1942. Although its performance was far from spectacular and it never saw combat, the type provided training for USAAF personnel and paved the way for development of high performance jet aircraft.** *AFFTC*

Below left: **On 14 October 1947 Capt Charles E 'Chuck' Yeager became the first human to travel faster than the speed of sound when he streaked above Rogers Dry Lake at Mach 1.06 (700mph) in the Bell X-1 rocket research aircraft. After the feared sound barrier was broken an informal competition sprang up between the USAF X-planes and the US Navy supersonic Skyrocket research aircraft. The Navy was first to make Mach 2 in November 1953, but Yeager soon took the improved X-1A to Mach 2.44.** *AFFTC*

Above right: **The XB-35 flying wing bomber, with contra-rotating propellers, photographed early in its flight test program at Edwards.** *AFFTC*

Right: **Members of the prestigious X-15 test team: Capt Joe Engle, Maj Robert A 'Bob' Rushworth, John B 'Jack' McKay (NASA), Maj William J 'Pete' Knight, Milt Thompson (NASA) and Bill Dana (NASA).** *AFFTC*

Bell test pilot Bob Stanley got airborne for the first 'official' flight, despite his having already been airborne during fast taxi trials over preceding days.

By now, this deserted corner of California had become the USAF Materiel Command (AFMC) Flight Test Facility, later to be known simply as North Base. Within a year Lockheed was here with its XP-80 and Muroc was gaining a name for itself as the place to test.

The single most famous event at what is now Edwards AFB was when Capt Charles E 'Chuck' Yeager became the first man to break the sound barrier, a remarkable feat accomplished in the bright orange Bell X-1 on the morning of 14 October 1947. This achievement confirmed the direction of aeronautical development and the future of military aviation.

The informal approach to flight safety during the late 1940s and early 1950s was a factor that lead to horrendous accident rates dur-

ing this period amongst the small team of heroic test pilots. The pilots flew an incredible number of new types and amassed an amazing number of sorties. Chuck Yeager was reputed to have once flown 27 different aircraft types in a single month. In 1948 a tragic 13 fatalities were recorded here. On 5 June 1948 Capt Glen Edwards and his colleagues were killed in the crash of their YB-49 jet derivative of the XB-35 flying wing bomber. In December 1949 the base was renamed in his honour and on 25 June 1951 the base became officially known as the USAF Flight Test Center (AFFTC).

Below: **Conceived as a Mach 3 interceptor, the YF-12 was a development of the awe-inspiring Lockheed SR-71A. The YF-12 never entered production but the SR-71 went on to have a remarkable career, plying its trade as a reconnaissance platform operating at altitudes in excess of 80,000ft.** *AFFTC*

Above: **Edwards today. Extensively tested at Edwards, the Lockheed Martin F-22A Raptor represents the future of manned air combat. This aircraft re-writes the air combat rulebook . Here 'Raptor 02' (4002 – second development aircraft) flies past the tower.** *AFFTC*

Below: **High above Rodgers Dry Lake, an F-16D of the 416th Flight Test Squadron (FLTS) based at Edwards. Note the runways marked out on the lakebed.** *AFFTC*

Reach for the sky. This gleaming Lockheed F-104 Starfighter is dramatically pole-mounted outside the USAF Test Pilots School at Edwards. *Jamie Hunter/AVIACOM*

LEARN TO TEST

Test Pilots School

Learning how to test aircraft became a serious and important business. In 1944 the USAAF Test Pilot School (TPS) was established at Wright-Patterson AFB in Ohio. As a natural progression it moved to the testing 'Mecca' at Edwards in 1951. The risk-filled early days are now long gone, but today's test pilots remain a rare and special breed, pushing the boundaries of aviation.

Under Col André Gerner, the commandant of TPS in 2005, Lt Col Eric Lagier was the deputy commander: 'When students first walk into the school we set about teaching them how an aeroplane flies, how fast, how high, how far. We cover basic aerodynamics, how to conduct testing for take-off and landing, energy concepts, all of these make up basic aircraft testing. This is covered with 57 hours of basic performance theory and 21 hours of flight time'.

Today's TPS at Edwards runs a number of courses tailored to specific requirement, however the 'bread and butter' remains the two long courses that run annually. This 48-week course teaches pilots, navigators and engineers everything they need to know about test-

ing. The school has always been pro-active with change and reacts to requirements from the front line; they even offer a course for the new generation of Unmanned Aerial Vehicle (UAV) testers.

As the USAF tests fewer 'all-new' aircraft, system testing is taking on increasing importance. The ability to test and evaluate new equipment for existing platforms, enhancing capabilities, is becoming one of the most important aspects of this demanding work. The test community is evolving to support rapid fielding techniques for new technology with emphasis placed on new doctrines such as network-centric warfare.

To complete its test tasks the USAF TPS at Edwards flies a number of aircraft types, mainly the T-38 Talon and the F-16 Fighting Falcon. Lt Col Lagier explained, 'We have the T-38 as a workhorse as well as the F-16 and the Beech C-12, we just lost the F-15 Eagle when Edwards lost all F-15 test operations to Eglin. About 2-3 months into the program we get the students to go out and put together a check profile to detail everything a particular aeroplane can do, within limits. This is the student's first major aerial test. We try to bring in an aeroplane that no one will have flown before. After this performance phase we look at flying qualities and get the stu-

Right: **Taxying onto the end of runway 22 at Edwards, this Lockheed Martin F-16B heads out for a TPS mission.** *Jamie Hunter/AVIACOM*

Centre right: **Framed by TPS F-16s the KC-10A tanker in the distance is deployed here to support F-22A testing.** *Jamie Hunter/AVIACOM*

Bottom right: **One of the school's workhorse Northrop T-38C Talons, equipped with a large instrumented boom, awaits its student and instructor in the late afternoon sun at Edwards.** *Jamie Hunter/AVIACOM*

dents to discover debilitating handling qualities of our aircraft. More and more these days we're not building new aeroplanes but we are modifying the old ones, consequently the systems phase is becoming one of the key points in the curriculum, we look at Electro-Optical and Infra-red systems, radars and weapons. The big one that is just kicking off is network-centric warfare and we are starting to teach how to go out and test it. New theories from the strategists are constantly being incorporated into what we do here'. Indeed, one of the latest developments is the AFFTC Flight Test University,

Below: **Pre-flight in the F-16 – a 'Viper' pilot prepares to head out from Edwards for a training mission.** *AFFTC*

Bottom: **Working the pattern at Edwards. A student tucks the gear as he gets to grips with the sporty Talon trainer.** *Jamie Hunter/AVIACOM*

Left: **TPS instructor pilots in an F-16B at Edwards.**
Jamie Hunter/AVIACOM

Below left: **A pair of TPS F-16Bs ease out to the
runway. Both of these aircraft are from a batch
of F-16s built for the Pakistan Air Force but
never delivered due to an arms embargo in
the 1990s. After many years in storage
some of the aircraft were delivered to the
USAF test fleet. The remainder were
delivered to the US Navy to operate as
adversary aircraft with NSAWC (Naval
Strike Air Warfare Center) at NAS
Fallon, NV.** *Jamie Hunter/AVIACOM*

Right: **Resplendent in its 412th Test Wing markings, an immaculate
F-16B attached to the Test Pilot School.** *Jamie Hunter/AVIACOM*

a new project at Edwards to act as a central area of excellence for
flight test and evaluation.

'The curriculum here has morphed over time. We used to go off
and fly sorties on another airplane and come back and write a formal report. We have changed that and now we do a week field trip
for the whole course rather than small groups.'

One of the key assets for the school is the Variable-stability
In-flight Simulator Test Aircraft (VISTA) NF-16D, a one-of-a-kind
F-16 that is primarily used for training in handling qualities. Lt Col
Lagier said, 'VISTA is basically an in-flight simulator. The front cockpit has a side stick and centre stick and once you are airborne you
can re-configure the jet to fly in different ways; like it has canards,
like a delta wing or make it like a large heavy airplane. Being an F-16
one can fly and manoeuvre it with abandon'.

The USAF TPS at Edwards attracts students from all over the
world, the waiting list is long and the competition for a place is
tough. For a pilot to gain a place they must have an exemplary
record and a minimum of 750 flight hours. 'The USAF overall is
downsizing, but there is no major outflow from the test community.
Our command here decided that manning levels were very important and we have 100% manning. We have a new UAV flight test
course that lasts three weeks. It started in May 2005 and the community is screaming for UAV test pilots. We are proud of producing
the best test pilots and navigators here.'

**High above the Mojave desert a TPS F-16B formates on a
KC-135R tanker. The brightly-painted F-16s are also used by the
445th FLTS for chase duties.** *AFFTC*

Above: **The Test Pilots School operates the VISTA NF-16D, which is a unique platform used to train pilots about different handling qualities. The aircraft is also used to evaluate new technology concepts.** *AFFTC*

Left: **This Talon can be identified as a T-38C thanks to the GPS antenna on the nose and the pilot's Head Up Display (HUD).** *Jamie Hunter/AVIACOM*

Below: **One of the C-12Cs operated by the 412th Test Wing at Edwards. The Test Pilots School uses the aircraft extensively during the year-long course.** *Jamie Hunter/AVIACOM*

Above: **T-38 instructor and student leave it to the last minute to close the 'lids' to prevent the cockpit getting too hot before getting airborne from a sweltering Edwards.** *Jamie Hunter/AVIACOM*

Below: **Cruising downwind for runway 22, this T-38C catches the golden afternoon light at Edwards. The T-38C features a host of new avionics as well as re-designed engine air intakes, it is also receiving new ejector seats.** *AFFTC*

Above: **The future is here. Lockheed Martin's F-22AA Raptor has been in flight test at Edwards since 1998.** *USAF/TSgt Ben Bloker*

Left: **Raptors 01 and 02 photographed over the Sierra Nevada near Edwards. These were the first two of nine flying EMD aircraft, with a further two used for static testing. Raptor 02 was used extensively for weapons trials at Edwards. Raptor 01 has now been retired and is in the USAF museum at Wright-Patterson AFB.** *USAF*

Bottom: **Raptor 4005 in the 'hot refuelling' pit at Edwards, demonstrating refuelling with engines running. Certification of 'hot refuelling' was expedited to overcome any tanker availability shortfalls that could have affected the test schedule.** *AFFTC*

THE SHARP END OF TESTING

Raptor CTF

The chance to climb into a new aeroplane and push it to the limits must be the ultimate dream for any test pilot. Few programs come along these days that allow such glory, however, there can be few places better than Edwards for this kind of work. In terms of fighters in the US, Lockheed Martin's F-22A Raptor and forthcoming F-35 Joint Strike Fighter (JSF) are strictly run programs but still involve taking a new type up and seeing what it can do.

Maj Sean Borror is a Raptor pilot with the 411th FLTS (Flight Test Squadron): 'I flew the F-16 on the front line and following the year at TPS I went across to the 416th FLTS to join the F-16 Combined Test Force (CTF) before moving down to the 411th, the F-22A Raptor CTF. I undertook my Raptor conversion academics down at Tyndall and the flying portion of my training here at Edwards. The 411th is like many of the CTFs and is comprised of a mix of military, government, civilian and contractor pilots, engineers and managers – we all work together.'

The Raptor CTF team at Edwards was, in September 2005, nearing the end of the exhaustive Engineering Manufacturing and Development (EMD) phase of the program. Maj Borror explained, 'The F-22 is a strange beast because we haven't yet got to the end of EMD but we already have operational squadrons standing up. We are finishing the last portion of EMD testing so Raptor can be declared operational in December 2005. The biggest portion is clearing the rest of the flight envelope, so there's a lot of loads testing going on and we are in the middle of a surge to be completed at the end of October 2005. We've almost completed the "clean" aircraft testing and we are getting ready to test the two-external-tank configuration, both envelope expansion and flutter testing, so the guys on the squadrons can go and fly the jet without too many limitations. The other effort we have ongoing is the supersonic JDAM (Joint Direct Attack Munition) separation tests to ensure the bomb can safely separate from the aircraft.'

Conceived as the Advanced Tactical Fighter (ATF) requirement to replace the F-15C Eagle, Raptor has come a long way since flight testing began at Edwards in May 1998. Lockheed Martin built nine flying EMD Raptors (and two static test airframes) to handle the brunt of the test and development work with the CTF there. The test program was executed as efficiently as possible with a joint industry/customer team at Edwards as they sought to expand the envelope and discover Raptor's true potential. From the outset it was clear that the aircraft had huge capability, with its supercruise performance (sustained supersonic speed without afterburner) a crucial strength. Lockheed Martin Chief Test pilot Paul Metz was

recorded as saying, 'Raptor can blast off supersonically from the deck. Level acceleration in military power or less is sprightly at altitudes, but astounding in full afterburner. Accelerating through Mach 1 in military power in the Raptor feels similar to accelerating in an F-15 in full afterburner.'

The stealthy Raptor was designed to ply its trade unhindered above the SAM networks of Cold War Europe and to operate when the B-2 and F-117, operating at night due to vulnerability to enemy fighters, could not. More importantly, Raptor is able to defend itself against fighters and thus operate around the clock with impunity, its stealthy characteristics keeping it hidden from other fighters to give it a 'first look, first shot' advantage. Its APG-77 Active Electronic Scanned Array (AESA) radar design helps reduce electronic emissions so as not to betray the fighter's position. Moreover, the pilot can actually turn the radar off and use its ALR-94 passive receiver system to track an emitting target and use the fighter datalink to receive information from other platforms, so it can essentially conduct a radar-silent attack. The intra-flight datalink can allow a Raptor that is outside its missile envelope to track a target and covertly send target data to a closer Raptor which can then make the silent kill on the unsuspecting enemy.

Despite these awesome capabilities, the aircraft has attracted its fair share of criticism with many arguing that the aircraft was conceived for a mission that no longer exists, not to mention its weighty $132m price tag per aircraft, without development costs factored. However those close to the program insist that it is living up to its revolutionary moniker and is a vital tool in the battle for the US to retain air dominance for the future. The aircraft's combination of stealthy characteristics, supercruise and advanced integrated avionics clearly give it the edge on everything else out there. However, despite testing having explored the true extent of its capabilities, much of this remains highly classified. This makes it hard for the USAF to shout too loudly about Raptor's successes despite the desire to secure political support for the program. Original plans to procure 648 production aircraft dwindled by early 2004 to a revised total of 224 aircraft following a spending cap of $36.8bn enforced by US Congress.

Early snags bought up by the test program included a performance shortfall by the new F119 engines and a realisation that

Lockheed Martin remained badly behind schedule. The knock-on effect of this was a delay to the start of Initial Operational Test and Evaluation (IOT&E) at Edwards from August 2002 to 29 April 2004, led by the 31st Test and Evaluation Squadron (TES) which is also based at Edwards. Once under way, this phase of testing involved six development F-22As flying 188 realistic simulated combat sorties in a number of scenarios, including escort missions with B-2s and F-117s, aerial engagements with aggressor F-16s from Nellis and demonstration of a basic air-to-surface capability. Delays in the start of IOT&E, however, served to compress the entire testing schedule as operational declaration, set in stone for December 2005, loomed. The decision had to be made to continue development testing (EMD) beyond the start of operational testing in order to meet targets, so the team at Edwards concentrated on essential test points to allow operational test to begin.

Every new weapon system the Air Force acquires must be formally evaluated before the system enters full-rate production. The tests are overseen by an independent agency – the Air Force Operational Test and Evaluation Center (AFOTEC) located at Kirtland AFB, NM. The results are reported to the Office of the Secretary of Defense and to Congress. The report includes a pass or fail grade for both the operational effectiveness and the suitability of the weapon system. The successful completion of IOT&E paved the way for Full-Rate Production (FRP) to be finally agreed on 18 April 2005, but the US Department of Defense had again moved to cut total procurement to about 180 aircraft, although the Air Force was still pushing hard to increase this number to the 381 aircraft it required. The IOT&E summary looked positive and concluded succinctly that 'Ground defences could not engage the F-22A, no adversaries could survive'.

Away from the political wrangling, the USAF has rapidly developed Raptor's repertoire and the fighter has moved towards being a multi-role platform rather than a pure 'air dominance' platform, now toting the GBU-32 JDAM and re-designated on 17 September 2002 from F-22 to F-22A. Weapons testing for certain platforms has increased at Edwards over recent years as portions of test programs remained here rather than re-locating to other more traditional weapons testing sites. Maj Borror explained, 'There are two

Left: **One of three avionics development aircraft, Raptor 4005 overflies the distinctive red Owens Lake on a test mission from Edwards.** *USAF*

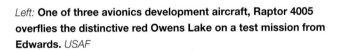

Above: **Raptor's low Radar Cross Section (RCS) is achieved with a combination of design, Radar Absorbent Structure (RAS) and radar absorbent coating. As the program has evolved, Raptors have changed camouflage schemes due to different applications of Radar Absorbent Material (RAM) and refining of the production standard finish. Electronic emissions and heat signature also play key roles in staying stealthy.** *AFFTC*

Top right: **An F-15D Eagle flies chase on Raptor 4002 during a flight envelope expansion mission. Testing Raptor's envelope saw testing at a wide range of altitudes and speeds to fully develop manoeuvrability. The red structure is the Spin Recovery Apparatus (SRA) which allows recovery from uncontrolled flight.** *USAF/AFFTC*

weight reduction steps had weakened the test airframes, resulting in much of the envelope expansion work being delayed until test aircraft Raptor 03 (4003) arrived in March 2000 – some nine months behind schedule. Following the slow delivery rates of the nine EMD test aircraft, the decision to proceed with Low Rate Initial Production (LRIP) had been threatened by Congress. However, a batch of eight aircraft was finally approved in 1999, known as Production Representative Test Vehicles (PRTV). As this batch of aircraft was ordered, the US Defense Acquisition Board set 'line in the sand' goals for the program to get back on track. With test points being achieved, the formal go-ahead for Lot 1 LRIP was approved in August 2001 and a further ten aircraft were ordered.

The test team had notched up some 2,000 flight test hours by 7 June 2002 but production and delivery of test aircraft from

Top: **Unlike the F-117 and B-2, Raptor is not confined to night operations to avoid marauding fighters. IOT&E concluded that 'Ground defences could not engage the F-22A and no adversaries could survive'.** *USAF*

Above: **Four EMD F-22As form up over the Mojave desert. The 411th FLTS Raptor CTF was nearing the end of the EMD phase in September 2005 ahead of Initial Operating Capability for the 1st Fighter Wing at Langley AFB in December 2005.** *USAF/Kevin Robertson*

Left: **Able to supercruise at high altitude, Raptor's Pratt & Whitney F119 engines also allow rapid acceleration in afterburner and vectored thrust to give the F-22A blistering all-round performance.** *USAF*

Left: **As well as its internal weapons bays, Raptor can be configured with four underwing pylons that can each carry a 2,200-litre drop tank and two AIM-120 AMRAAMs, making for an impressive load. However, external storage greatly compromises Raptor's stealthy characteristics and would likely only be used for ferry purposes.** *Lockheed Martin*

Below: **An F-22A flown by Maj John Teichert of the 411th FLTS releases a GBU-32 1,000 lb JDAM during supersonic release trials near the Panamint Range in 2005.** *USAF/Darin Russell*

Below: **Raptor 02 fired the first AIM-9 Sidewinder missile on 25 July 2000 as weapons separation trials commenced to evaluate firing air-to-air missiles from the internal weapons bays. Raptors continue to employ the AIM-9M ahead of future deployment of AIM-9X.** *USAF/Judson Brohmer*

Bottom: **Sidewinder firing expanded to include firing whilst manoeuvring. All conceivable flight regimes were tested. Raptor 02 is seen here at 40,000ft and a 26° angle-of-attack. Raptor began formal Initial Operational Test and Evaluation (IOT&E) at Edwards in April 2004 to evaluate the aircraft's lethality, survivability, deployability and maintainability in a variety of operational missions ahead of Operational Test and Evaluation at Nellis AFB.** *USAF/Judson Brohmer*

types of weapons release testing, you have pure separation and loads testing, for the F-16 most of that goes on down at Eglin. So they'll go out with a brand new bomb and will make sure that the loads on the aircraft don't exceed the limits for the Seek Eagle office. We'll then get it and handle the avionics portion of the work, making sure the correct co-ordinates are going from the computer in the aircraft to the bomb so that it is targeted accurately. For the F-16 the airframe and loads and weapons separation testing goes on at Eglin and primarily avionics and engine testing is conducted at Edwards. For the F-22A we're the only game in town in terms of developmental test (DT) and we do everything here at Edwards. The 422nd TES at Nellis is engaged in the follow-on test and evaluation (FOT&E) phase and after EMD finishes here Raptor will go into the same sort of cycle of improvement you see for other types such as F-16. In fact the CTF has already contracted and we have Raptors 2, 6 and 8 for loads envelope expansion, while aircraft 7 and 9 are our avionics test birds.'

Like all new complex aeroplanes, the road to operational capability has been beset with challenges for the team developing this impressive beast, but having carved out a niche for itself to operate as part of the integrated Global Strike Task Force (GSTF) its future is assured. The type's spiral development modernisation process will ensure that the aircraft receives emerging weapons and sensors, such as the Small Diameter Bomb (SDB), as they become available. Raptor doesn't carry electro-optic sensors or a targeting pod, but relies on target location information datalinked from other aircraft for its ground-attack mission. The aircraft's primary air-to-air weapons are the AIM-9M Sidewinder and the AIM-120C AMRAAM. Weapons are normally carried in the internal weapons bays and the landmark first AIM-120C test launch was achieved on 24 October 2000. It was the first of an incredible 60 planned 'shots'

Above left: **A pair of 416th FLTS F-16s with ALQ-167 radar jamming pods head back to Edwards with an F-22A following a test mission to simulate radar jamming scenarios against the Raptor in simulated engagements.** *AFFTC*

from all conceivable orientations. Weapons testing at Edwards was reported as having proceeded smoothly with few hitches, with launches executed in every conceivable situation. The AIM-120 is clearly the Raptor's primary weapon, arguably its pilots don't want to get in the situation where a close-in turning fight is necessary, not that anyone is in doubt as to its prowess in this environment – Raptor turns on the proverbial dime. As already detailed, Raptor's sensor fusion allows it to operate silently and it kills from long range. Consequently the decision to defer integration of the Joint Helmet-Mounted Cueing System (JHMCS) is not seen as a major hindrance for pilots.

TESTING THE FUTURE TODAY

The 412th TW Operations Group (OG) at Edwards oversees all testing here. Commanded by Col Christopher Cook it makes for quite a mission: 'I am responsible for all flying operations here at Edwards that are conducted as part of test, except for NASA test operations. I also have a couple of detachments that fall under my jurisdiction; one at Kirtland AFB for the "Big Crow" mission and also a group in the depot at Robins AFB flying the C-5 Galaxy (detachment of 418th FLTS). I have ten flight test squadrons including the 452nd and the new Joint Strike Fighter CTFs. The UAVs are starting to pick up a larger presence here and we have an enormous diversity, about 30 aeroplane types, under my control. I am a flight test navigator by trade and flew strategic bombers operationally, B-52s and FB-111 as a WSO before I came here to test pilot school. The USAF had me targeted for the B-2 originally but I got diverted to work in the "black world" and I worked on stealthy cruise missiles. I later flew the B-2 and I am one of the few WSOs that have done that. Back in the 1980s when I first came here there was a strong development test (DT) and operational test (OT) presence. Back then at TPS we used to get our hands slapped when we wrote up a development test and included operational aspects of that system. They'd say, "No, does it meet specification? Don't tell us if it will be good in a war." But there was a shift about the 1988-89 timeframe to move the opera-

Top: **Eagle testing is no longer conducted at Edwards, except for some engine work. The former Edwards F-15s have been transferred to Eglin for all development testing with the 40th FLTS. Here, Lt Col Troy Fontaine and Maj Kevin Steffenson are seen dropping five JDAMs on the China Lake test range on five separate, pre-planned targets.** *AFFTC*

Left: **Pole position – the 412th TW headquarters is impressively 'guarded' by these immaculate fighters: an F-16B and F-86.** *Jamie Hunter/AVIACOM*

tional view back further in the timeline to ensure what we do develop is useful. That has continued and today all our test forces are combined test forces. Our flightline doesn't have the diversity or as many aeroplanes that it had before, but we have some real valuable assets and the focus on safety and effectiveness has to be driven home.

412th Test Wing
Air Force Material Command (AFMC)

The 412th Test Wing at Edwards AFB comprises the following test squadrons:

410th FLTS	F-117A CTF (Plant 42 Palmdale)
411th FLTS	F-22A CTF
412th FLTS	'Speckled Trout'
416th FLTS	F-16/T-38 CTF
418th FLTS	Heavy aircraft and MV-22 CTF
419th FLTS	Bomber CTF
445th FLTS	Test support
452nd FLTS	ABL and UAV CTF. Predator Det at El Mirage
(370th FLTS)	AFRC test support

In addition, the JSF CTF will be standing up in 2006.

'We've got some programs out on the flight line right now that are on TSPR (Total System Performance Responsibility) – that means the contractor has total responsibility for the performance. This causes a clash of cultures when the program comes here as we have to review everything before it can enter testing here.' The USAF is now looking to move away from the TSPR concept.

'Our test ranges are national assets and the latest base realignment and closure underlined how these need to be managed and resourced so we can build the new technology. We have a lot of exciting stuff going on here with hypersonic flight and this kind of testing requires huge swathes of airspace because they are moving so fast. Shooting one-time-use vehicles out over the ocean becomes very expensive very quickly so we need to have corridors and instrument them appropriately. There are a lot of fascinating things going on and we have the responsibility to be ready to test these new platforms. Is there still an unknown out there?...You bet there is. There is still a demon out there and we have to be careful to identify where it is and not get bitten. We nearly had that recently. We had an F-22A that had a wake encounter behind an aircraft and had some very high gain activity in the flight control system that resulted in a very violent manoeuvre. The software saw a high angle of attack build up and then over-corrected and they got a large 'G-spike'. As aeroplanes go faster and weapons get smaller, it gets harder. Following the first Gulf War we have really focused on the warfighter. Most test pilots today have been in combat and the reason they became a test pilot

The flying antenna testbed C-135E is playing a big role in development and integration of battlefield information networks and communications nodes. The aircraft supports airborne communications transition to production and fusion into new command and control networks. The USAF Research Laboratory's (AFRL) C-135E testbed Command, Control, Communications, Computers and Intelligence (C4I) Airborne Testbed (ACAT) is seen here at Edwards.
Jamie Hunter/AVIACOM

Stealth on test

Above: **The USAF Lockheed Martin F-117A Nighthawk Combined Test Force (CTF) is the 410th FLTS, based at USAF Plant 42 at Palmdale. Integration of new GPS-guided weapons started in earnest on 21 January 2004 at the Precision Impact Range Area at Edwards AFB when YF-117A (serial 79-0784/ED) released two types of 2,000 lb JDAM. The variants used on this test were the GBU-31(v)1/B and the GBU-31(v)3/B. The GBU-31(v)1/B is based on the Mk 84 bomb and is used for its large blast and explosive force. The GBU-31(v)3/B is a BLU-109 variant used to penetrate hardened targets. This effort was part of the F-117 Block II, a software upgrade that updates the F-117 Operational Flight Program (OFP) to integrate advanced weapons, including the Enhanced GBU-27 (EGBU-27), JDAM and Wind Corrected Munitions Dispenser (WCMD). Hardware upgrades, including a MIL-STD-1760 compatible Stores Management Processor (SMP), are also being introduced. The Block II software upgrade was planned to complete testing in August 2005.** *AFFTC/Bobbi Garcia*

Above: **The 410th FLTS at Palmdale operates three early YF-117A Nighthawks. These aircraft are heavily involved in the Combat Capability Sustainment Program (CSSP) to introduce new capabilities for the future.** *Lockheed Martin*

was because they want to make better equipment for the combat air force. We do quite a lot of classified work here; we have certain technologies that we don't want to give away.'

One of the most important units here is the 445th FLTS; this squadron was previously known as 'Test Operations' and was reactivated in March 2004. The squadron was re-activated to consolidate the test support fleet under operational control, to provide post test pilot school training and to consolidate all test support under a single squadron. The 445th is an all-round test unit and has recently been heavily involved supporting the Royal Australian AF Wedgetail Airborne Early Warning and Control version of the Boeing 737 providing target aircraft for the new systems to track. It also supplies photo chase aircraft and has a KC-135R with an instrumented refuelling boom and sprayer for icing trials. In 2005 the squadron operated an F-16 with AGTS (aerial gunnery target system) to help test the Israeli 'Peace Marble' F-16I.

The commander of the 412th TW in 2005 was Col Joseph Lanni, a hugely experienced USAF experimental test pilot with over 4,300 flying hours in over 70 different aircraft types. As well as having previously been Director of the F-22A Combined Test Force at Edwards, Col Lanni was also commander of the Classified Flight Test Squadron from July 1995 to June 1997. During his tenure here Col Lanni flew the first flights of two highly classified prototypes, one being the still undisclosed YF-24 according to his biography. Details of this highly secretive unit are vague but it is understood to be an element of the AFFTC's Detachment 3 at the secret Groom Lake base in Nevada. The 'Classified FLTS' continues to conduct super-secret testing of some of the most advanced aerospace technology in the world today and is manned by the USAF's top experimental pilots flying some of the most exciting and intriguing missions.

VIPER VENOM

One of the largest Combined Test Forces (CTFs) at Edwards is that of the Lockheed Martin F-16 – the 416th FLTS. Capt Mike Presnar is a flight test engineer with the 416th: 'Most of our F-15 test work has moved to Eglin and we mainly deal with F-16 testing here now at Edwards. The M4.2+ Operational Flight Program (OFP) is our latest priority at the squadron and this is the latest avionics standard for the Block 50 F-16 under the Common Configuration Implementation Program (CCIP). We also have the European Partner Air Force (EPAF) Mid-Life Upgrade (MLU) team working here and we have Norwegian, Danish and Dutch pilots that also fly with us. The MLU and CCIP avionics upgrade tapes are similar, but separate efforts. We also currently have Chilean and Israeli programs running so we have to maintain a high level of security at the squadron.'

The Chilean Air Force F-16 work at the 416th is part of the 'Peace Puma' deal with Lockheed Martin for the Block 52M variant. In 2005, the test force at Edwards was tasked with preparing the aircraft for delivery, evaluating system performance on behalf of the customer nation as well as integrating JDAM and the Litening II targeting pod onto the type as well as the Rafael Python IV missile. 'Peace Marble V' is the current Israeli AF/DF F-16I program and was nearing completion at Edwards in 2005. The sophisticated F-16I is bristling with equipment and capabilities, with the CTF overseeing the introduction of colour moving map, JDAM, AMRAAM, LANTIRN and Litening II targeting pods as well as airframe performance at high operational gross weights. Oman and Poland are additional F-16 customers, with the Omani customer-specific electronic warfare (EW) suites amongst new systems that require testing.

The F-16 CTF was, in 2005, heavily involved in the USAF's accelerated R7 STING (Smart Targeting and Identification via Networked Geolocation) upgrade for

AFOTEC

The Air Force Operational Test and Evaluation Center (AFOTEC) is an independent USAF test agency responsible for testing new systems and assesses their capability to meet USAF needs by planning, executing, and reporting independent operational evaluations. From concept development through system employment, AFOTEC provides effectiveness, suitability, and operational impact expertise in the battlespace environment. Established on 1 January 1974 at Kirtland AFB, NM, AFOTEC came about due to shortfalls in US equipment deployed in Southeast Asia during the Vietnam conflict. Studies indicated that 21 of 22 major systems deployed in that theatre suffered major deficiencies in the field. AFOTEC was established to plan and conduct realistic, objective, and impartial operational test and evaluation to determine the operational effectiveness and suitability of Air Force systems and their capacity to meet mission needs.

Seek Eagle

The USAF Seek Eagle office (AFSEO) exists to improve the combat capability of USAF combat forces. The Seek Eagle program office oversees and certifies all weapons, tanks and pods carried externally or internally for safe carriage, employment, jettison, safe escape, and ballistic accuracy verification.

Top: **The 416th FLTS F-16 CTF at Edwards has been heavily involved in clearing new weapons for the type. This test shows a 2,000 lb JDAM being dropped.** *USAF*

Above: **The 416th fired the newest variant of the AIM-9 Sidewinder missile for the first time from an F-16 on 9 April 2004. Maj Ray Toth and Capt Nick Hague are seen here firing the AIM-9X.** *AFFTC/Tom Reynolds*

Above: **As part of the huge USAF F-16 Common Configuration Implementation Program (CCIP) the 416th FLTS has been constantly testing new equipment and software. The M4.1A+ update for the Block 40/42 F-16 introduce Link-16 datalink and the Joint Helmet-Mounted Cueing System (JHMCS) as well as the GBU-38 500 lb JDAM and the Lockheed Martin Sniper advanced targeting pod. The primary focus of this upgrade is the air-to-ground mission and M4.1A+ OFP software also ties in new fire-control computers and colour multi-function displays (MFDs).**
Jamie Hunter/AVIACOM

the ASQ-213 HARM Targeting System (HTS) pod on the Block 50/52 F-16CJ. Expected to enter service in September 2006, trials involve a pair of aircraft from the squadron as well as F-16CJs from the South Carolina Air National Guard in integrated development and operational testing. The new system upgrades the Suppression of Enemy Air Defence (SEAD) capabilities, allowing the F-16 to data share with the Link 16 datalink to network several HTS pods and locate emitters with greater accuracy while also generating target co-ordinates accurate enough to employ GPS-guided munitions such as the JDAM.

Above right: **A Block 42 F-16CG toting an impressive load of Wind Corrected Munitions Dispensers (WCMD), AIM-9X and AIM-120 AMRAAMs.** *AFFTC*

Right: **Sitting in a Block 40 F-16, this 416th Viper test pilot wears the impressive new Joint Helmet Cueing System (JHMCS). This helmet is now in production and is operational on US fighters, allowing the pilot to cue sensors and weapons such as the AIM-9X by looking at the target.** *Jamie Hunter/AVIACOM*

The F-16 CTF at Edwards pulled out all the stops to accelerate testing of the 500 lb GBU-38 JDAM. Developmental and Operational testing was completed in just 30 days to initially clear the new weapon for the Block 30 F-16. A similar effort integrated the Litening II targeting pod on Block 50 F-16s with the 416th FLTS condensing six weeks of developmental test and evaluation into three and a half days to verify the M3.1B+ software upgrade.
Jamie Hunter/AVIACOM

FUTURE FIGHTER – JSF

The Joint Strike Fighter program is what Edwards is all about, taking a new system and testing every single element. The System Development and Demonstration (SDD) phase of the JSF program started in October 2001 when Lockheed Martin got the green light for its F-35 design following a fly-off against Boeing's X-32, much of which took place at Edwards. The competition had been fierce, with Lockheed Martin's family of X-35 demonstrators pushed to the limits by the test team at Edwards, Palmdale and across at NAS Patuxent River, MD. The aircraft is currently planned to be produced in conventional take-off and landing (CTOL), carrier-based (CV) and short take-off vertical-land (STOVL) multi-role fighter variants. The latter is the preferred option for the US Marines, the United Kingdom and has also now been selected by the USAF. The nature of the program and its multi-national involvement means that the test team will be diverse, with a number of project pilots and engineers from partner nations. With the first flight for the first SDD production representative F-35 slated for 2006 the test team is already gearing up at Edwards. The SDD phase will initially see fourteen fully-instrumented flight test examples built by Lockheed Martin at its Fort Worth plant. This will comprise five USAF conventional F-35A versions, four STOVL F-35Bs and five US Navy (CV) F-35Cs to undertake safety and effectiveness testing and to verify the aircraft. The JSF CTF at Edwards is planned to receive its first F-35A in September 2006 and could eventually grow to operate as many as 28 aircraft. Across at Patuxent River the majority of the F-35C carrier and F-35B VSTOL portion of the work will be conducted by the US Navy and US Marine Corps.

From the very start, JSF was ambitious, and Edwards played a key role in turning the ambition into reality. If it lives up to expectation it promises to be the most important combat aircraft program in the world, with the latest technology rolled into an affordable combat aircraft for nations around the globe.

The arrival of the System Development and Demonstration phase of the Lockheed Martin F-35 Joint Strike Fighter (JSF) program in 2006 will herald the start of a major new test project.
Lockheed Martin

Left: **With photo-chase F-16B in tow, the Lockheed Martin X-35C carrier version heads back to Edwards during the competition fly-off against Boeing's X-32. The F-35C is intended to replace the F/A-18C/D Hornet in US Navy service.** *Lockheed Martin*

Bottom left: **The X-35A demonstrated in-flight refuelling capability from the 412th TW's NKC-135E on its 10th test flight with Lt Col Paul Smith at the controls.** *Lockheed Martin*

Right: **Seen here over Edwards, Lockheed Martin built three X-35 Concept Demonstrator Aircraft (CDA), with the first being the X-35A that made its maiden flight on 24 October 2000 from Palmdale to Edwards with Lockheed Martin X-35 test pilot Tom Morgenfeld at the helm.** *Lockheed Martin*

Left: **Dennis O'Donoghue lands at Edwards following Boeing's X-32B concept demonstrator's first sortie on 29 March 2001. The X-32B had already been tested over the hover pit at Palmdale from 7 March 2001 to simulate hovering in free air. The aircraft then entered a four-month test program to validate Boeing's direct-lift approach to Short Take-off and Vertical Landing (STOVL) flight. Boeing lost out to Lockheed Martin in the 'winner takes all' JSF competition.** *AFFTC*

Below: **Head to head. The two JSF candidate concept demonstrator aircraft; the Boeing X-32 and Lockheed Martin X-35. With the award of the System Development and Demonstration phase of the contract awarded to Lockheed Martin, JSF testing at Edwards is set to resume in 2006.** *Lockheed Martin*

HEAVY DUTY

The 418th FLTS at Edwards conducts testing for heavy tanker-transport aircraft types such as the C-130 Hercules and KC-135 Stratotanker. The squadron also supports the ongoing CV-22 Osprey test effort at Edwards for USAF Special Operations Command (AFSOC).

Above: **The USAF Special Operations Command CV-22 Osprey program is currently engaged in developmental testing at Edwards AFB, CA, which will be followed by Initial Operational Test and Evaluation (IOT&E) and an operational utility evaluation in 2006. The Osprey Integrated Test Team is part of the 418th FLTS, Maj James Donald, Defense Contract Management Command acceptance test pilot for the CV-22 said, 'The CV-22 is beneficial to AFSOC (AF Special Operations Command) because it combines the best capabilities of both the C-130 and the MH-53 Pave Low. The CV-22 allows you to go twice as far as the Pave Low and gives you more landing capabilities than the C-130.' CV-22 testing at Edwards should be complete during 2007 when test operations will switch to Hurlburt Field at Eglin AFB, FL, and Kirtland AFB, NM.** *Jamie Hunter/AVIACOM*

Above left: **The first Production Representative Test Vehicle (PRTV) CV-22 arrived at Edwards in September 2005 and the Air Force Operational Test and Evaluation Center (AFOTEC) and AFSOC will test the aircraft and then conduct Operational Utility Evaluation. The second PRTV was scheduled to arrive at Edwards in late 2005 as operational testing gets into full swing. Following this, both PRTVs will transition to Kirtland to stand-up the first USAF CV-22 training squadron.** *AFFTC*

Left: **A close-up view of the CV-22. The CV-22 features a Multi-Mode Radar (MMR) for ultra-low terrain-hugging operations for penetration missions, Directed Infra-Red Countermeasures (DIRCM) and a retractable in-flight refuelling probe. AFSOC is expecting to receive 50 CV-22s, with initial operational capability (IOC) set for 2009.** *Jamie Hunter/AVIACOM*

Right: **A Boeing C-17A Globemaster undergoing testing in the Benefield Anechoic Facility at Edwards during electromagnetic interference and electromagnetic compatibility testing.** *AFFTC*

Left: **The 418th FLTS retains a C-17A for development testing and integration testing of new systems. The C-17 is one of the first platforms to receive the new Northrop Grumman large aircraft self-protection systems (LAIRCM).** *AFFTC*

Centre left: **The Lockheed Martin C-130J has completed most of the test work undertaken at Edwards with load dropping trials now certified. This example is photographed in the Benefield Anechoic Facility.** *AFFTC*

Below: **The 418th FLTS commenced risk-reduction flight testing for the USAF C-130 Avionics Modernisation Program (AMP) on an MC-130E in 2005. The MC-130E is loaned from the 919th SOW and the flights are being conducted to determine the performance of the new terrain-following radar. The Boeing-led AMP includes a new glass cockpit with head-up display (HUD). For the MC-130E it also includes a new radome housing modern multifunction radar and a new communications systems to comply with Global Air Traffic Management avionics.** *Jamie Hunter/AVIACOM*

BOMBER COUNTRY

Where is the one place in the US that one can find all three USAF strategic bombers? Edwards of course. The 419th FLTS here is the Global Power Bomber CTF, and it flies not only the B-1 Lancer and B-2 Spirit but also the stalwart B-52 Stratofortress. Carl Dane is the deputy commander here; he is a civilian flight test engineer with a huge amount of experience: 'We have 650 people here on the CTF. We have two B-52Hs, two B-1Bs and a B-2A, which is permanently loaned from the 509th Bomb Wing at Whiteman. Our maintenance guys are triple qualified and work on all three aircraft. We also support the 31st TES operational test and AFOTEC missions here for our bombers. Our B-2 is in a sustaining phase for the fleet. We are engaged in radar upgrades and we are also introducing new weapons for the type. We have recently completed Link-16 datalink integration and we are now looking at the Network Centric (Net-Centric) capabilities we need to introduce for the B-1 and B-52.' In 2005 the B-2 radar modernisation team passed a final design review by the USAF and delivered the first upgraded test radar for integration, test and software development. Northrop Grumman, prime contractor for the overall B-2 program, also leads the radar-modernisation team that includes Raytheon, the radar-system provider. The effort will replace the current antenna with an active, electronically scanned array (AESA) antenna. In July 2005 Raytheon delivered the first APQ-181 AESA radar to replace the current mechanically scanned antennas with faster and more-reliable solid-state arrays. This is part of a $382m effort to install six radars on operational B-2s before production for the entire B-2 fleet.

'The B-1 has completed the Conventional Munitions Upgrade (CMUP) and is now getting a software upgrade, the Fully Integrated Datalink (FIDL) and is getting fit checked for the Small Diameter Bomb (SDB) and the Sniper targeting pod on an external mount. The B-52 is also getting Sniper and we are just finishing off the software phase of the AMI (Avionics Mid-life Improvement).' Also on the cards for the B-52 is the electronic attack mission. The B-52 Stand-Off Jammer (SOJ), or EB-52 is likely to play a large role in operations for the 419th at Edwards over coming years as the venerable 'BUFF' takes on this new role.'

Left: **The ultimate symbol of Global Power, a Northrop Grumman B-2A Spirit of the 419th FLTS unleashes an impressive load of 500 lb GBU-38 JDAMs on the Utah test range near Hill AFB during a test mission from Edwards.** *AFFTC*

Above: **In December 2004 the 419th FLTS flew B-2A Spirit Link-16 datalink integration test missions from Edwards. The addition of Link-16 allows battlefield information to be transferred and shared between platforms and also with ground forces. Maj Jeff Warmka of the 419th FLTS said, 'Since Operation *Allied Force*, USAF leadership has clearly articulated a vision of getting real-time information into the cockpit. Although the B-2A was designed for strategic strikes well forward of the battle lines, Link-16 now gives commanders in large-scale regional conflicts the ability to reach out and task B-2As within the battle area.'** *AFFTC/Bobbi Garcia*

Below: **The 419th FLTS B-2A 'Spirit of New York' on its landing roll at Edwards following a test mission here in October 2005.** *Wesley Turner*

Top right: **The B-1B Lancer team at Edwards has been conducting integration of the AGM-154 Joint Stand-off Weapon (JSOW) and AGM-158 Joint Air-to-Surface Stand-off Missile (JASSM) in a further phase of the Conventional Munitions Upgrade Program (CMUP). Seen here dropping a JASSM Separation Test Vehicle (STV) on the NAWS China Lake test ranges, the B-1 has the unique ability to re-plan the JASSM after launch and re-program the route of each individual weapon while in flight. Compatibility between JSOW, JASSM and JDAM will enable the B-1 to carry a mixed load in the weapons bay.** *AFFTC*

Centre right: **The B-52H was gearing up to take on a new role as a Stand-Off Jammer (SOJ). Testing for this new mission was to play a large role in operations for the 419th FLTS at Edwards until it was cancelled in 2006.** *AFFTC*

Right: **The B-52H is receiving the capability to use new weapons and sensors to make it a potent battlefield support platform. This Operational Test (OT) B-52H attached to the 31st TES at Edwards is seen dropping a JDAM from its internal weapons bay during 2005.** *AFFTC*

THE FUTURE IS HERE

Arguably one of the most revolutionary and exciting missions at Edwards falls to the 452nd FLTS. Lt Col Doug Jaquish is the squadron commander here: 'My role here is to make sure we conduct safe, effective flight test to get UAVs, Global Hawk, Predator, and J-UCAS (Joint-Unmanned Combat Air System), tested and proven so we can get new capability into the field and understand these new capabilities. We also take ideas from the field and see how we can improve what we have. These systems are not as mature as they usually are in a production sense, so we are trying to catch up. We have development roadmaps for the Global Hawk and Predator and a lot of this is tied to putting capability out there in a preliminary form, what we call advanced concept technology demonstrators. So when we want to go ahead with production, we have to take the capability and make sure it is suitable for production. In the current environment we depend a lot on contractor logistical support, but we are working toward doing maintenance ourselves. With Global Hawk we are wringing out production sensor suites, the integrated sensor suite comes from the vendor and we are making sure they are meeting standard for collection that we want on the Global Hawk. We are also looking at the ability for a UAV to operate in international airspace as well as more basic handling characteristics like crosswind limit testing with UAV test pilots. We are also looking at digital engine control, trying to improve engine performance and increase service ceiling for Global Hawk.

'As regards MQ-1 Predator, we are adding new weapons and sensors to the aircraft, although we don't fly the type from here but from a remote location to use the Edwards and China Lake ranges.' The pre-production General Atomics MQ-9A Predator B, a larger

The Boeing YAL-1A Airborne Laser (ABL) is a huge program at Edwards. ABL consists of a high-energy chemical oxygen iodine laser (COIL) carried aboard a modified Boeing 747-400F. The ABL platform is capable of autonomously locating and tracking enemy ballistic missiles in the boost phase of flight, then accurately firing the high-energy laser to destroy them near their launch area. *AFFTC*

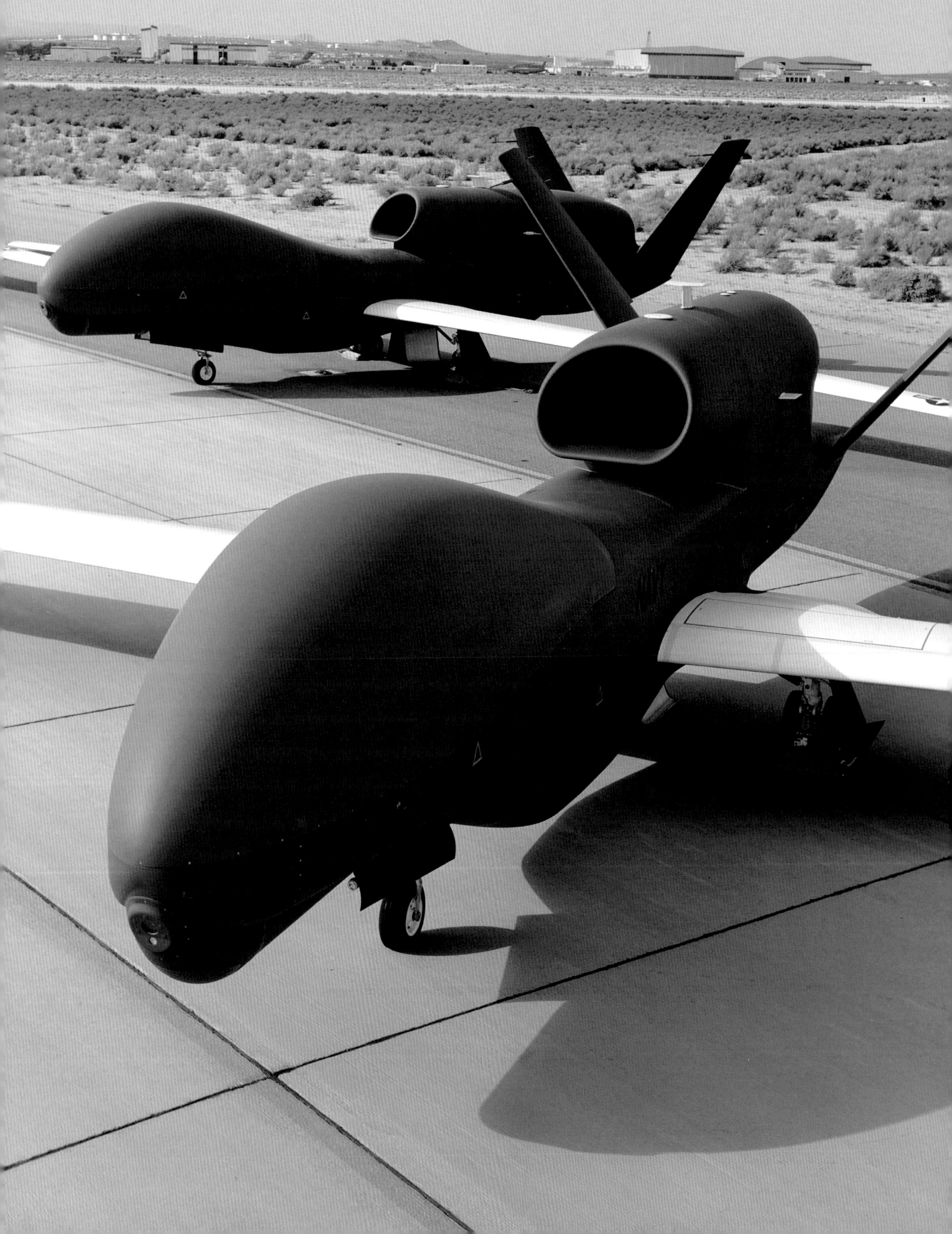

Left: **A pair of RQ-4A Global Hawks on the south base ramp at Edwards. Northrop Grumman expected to fly its improved RQ-4B Global Hawk in early 2006. The new variant has increased fuselage length and wingspan to permit carriage of greater sensor payloads to undertake a wider variety of missions, whilst utilising the same powerplant. The Global Hawk program has now been split down into Blocks. The original RQ-4As are now known as Block 10, with Blocks 20, 30 and 40 being the change to the RQ-4B, reflecting payload configurations.** *AFFTC*

Right: **An early RQ-4A turns final at Edwards during testing.** *AFFTC*

variant of the original MQ-1 Predator, has already been in limited operational use in combat theatres since August 2004. MQ-9A operates as a 'hunter-killer' platform at medium altitude, with plans to operate four examples ready for official operational employment by March 2006 equipped to carry the 500 lb GBU-38 JDAM as well as the 500 lb GBU-12 laser-guided bomb (LGB) that it has already been cleared to carry. As well as its existing six examples, the USAF has ordered an additional 13 MQ-9s as it works towards an operational fleet of 60 UCAVs with two dedicated squadrons as well as a mixed MQ-9A/MQ-1 unit.

One of the most exciting new UAV programs is J-UCAS (Joint Unmanned Combat Air Systems). This is a joint DARPA, USAF and US Navy effort designed to 'demonstrate the technical feasibility, military utility and operational value for a networked system of high performance, weaponised UAVs to effectively and affordably prosecute 21st century combat missions, including Suppression of Enemy Air Defenses (SEAD), surveillance, and precision strike within the emerging global command and control architecture'. J-UCAS combined the USAF's Unmanned Combat Air Vehicle (UCAV) and US Navy UCAV-N programs. The latter centred upon the Northrop Grumman X-47A that was tested extensively at NAWS China Lake, CA. Having completed 64 flights, the Boeing X-45A formed the USAF part of the program and concluded its flight test program at Edwards in August 2005. In the final demonstration mission two X-45As detected multiple simulated threats, replanned attacks due to operator target priorities; and performed a co-ordinated strike. The X-45A team worked under the careful oversight of NASA's Dryden Flight Research Center, Edwards, as well as the 452nd FLTS, successfully demonstrating release of a GPS-guided weapon, multi-vehicle operations and in-flight transfer of operator control of two air vehicles to another control station nearly 900 miles away during beyond-line-of-sight flight operations. Lt Col Jaquish commented, 'We are at a point now where Boeing and Northrop Grumman are developing the upscale version of J-UCAS and the manufacturers are looking at sets of requirements for DARPA, USAF and the US Navy and we are standing up facilities for flight testing over the next 2-3 years here. We will fly the missions here to prove out the new capabilities and take it from the end of the previous testing to demonstrating the new X-45C that Boeing is building. The common operating system will involve some co-operation between

Boeing's X-45A of the Joint Unmanned Combat Air Systems (J-UCAS) team flew extensively from Edwards including a mission that transferred aircraft control from a pilot at NASA Dryden to another pilot at Boeing's Seattle facility. The Block 4 software upgrade allowed the UAV to fly autonomously in co-ordinated flights while engaging multiple targets. *AFFTC*

the two manufacturers with the same software, but the two contractors are looking to co-develop a common system'. As well as Boeing's X-45C, Northrop Grumman is developing the X-47B, both of which will prove out differing criteria. These range from low-observability to carrier suitability for the Navy, even autonomous air refuelling. J-UCAS is set to revolutionise future air combat, and as Lt Col Jaquish commented, 'F-35 will be the last manned fighter'.

Another key program at the squadron is the YAL-1A Airborne Laser (ABL). This is a 90% contractor team but with the USAF keeping a keen eye on technical and safety points. 'The project is back in a passive phase and is getting modified ready for the laser installation. We will then prove out the modifications and track and find targets. The testing will culminate with live target shots in 2008.' Exciting times are clearly ahead for this CTF as it takes the USAF forward and stays at the sharp end of flight testing with revolutionary new aerospace platforms.

NASA DRYDEN

Some of the most innovative and interesting flight research studies conducted at Edwards are conducted along the flightline at the National Aeronautics and Space Administration (NASA) Dryden Flight Research Center here. Dryden is NASA's centre for aeronautical flight research and atmospheric flight operations and studies advanced aeronautics and space and related technologies. It also serves as a back-up landing site for the Space Shuttle and numerous projects here to validate design concepts and systems used in development and operation of the Orbiters. The history of Dryden dates back as early as Chuck Yeager's Bell X-1 flights and has gone on to include ground-breaking programs such as the F-16XL test-bed, used to test Digital Flight Control Systems (DFCS) and a project to improve laminar airflow on aircraft flying at sustained supersonic speeds. The F-18 Hornet High Angle-of-Attack Research Vehicle (HARV) flew until September 1996 and demonstrated stabilised flight at angles of attack between 65 and 70 degrees using thrust vectoring vanes.

NASA Dryden has operated a unique blend of weird and wonderful aircraft throughout its existence and continues the tradition of advanced flight research at this historic base in California.

Above: **NASA's beautiful NB-52B Stratofortress was finally retired in late 2004 having become synonymous with flight research at Edwards, having played key roles in early lifting body tests, the X-15 program and later being heavily involved with the X-43A hypersonic scramjet. The NB-52 first arrived at Edwards for the USAF on 8 June 1959 and was permanently loaned to NASA from April 1976. The NB-52 served as the launch 'mothership' for the X-15's 199 flights and later for the X-43A (carried here) during its Mach 10 record-setting flight on 16 November 2004.** *AFFTC*

Chapter Two
Eglin Testers

Sharpening the Sword

Located near some of the most beautiful beaches and most popular tourist resorts in the United States, Eglin AFB is a huge facility on the sun-kissed Gulf Coast of Florida's Panhandle. The base here traces its roots back to 1931 when the Army Air Corps Tactical School saw the potential of the sparsely populated forested areas and the vast expanse of the adjacent Gulf of Mexico for use as a gunnery and bombing range.

Today, Eglin is one of the largest air bases in the world, covering some 724 square miles of reservation and 123,000 square miles of ranges out to sea in the Gulf Test Range. Eglin is home to a diversity of development flight testing met by the resident Air Armament Center, part of

Air Force Materiel Command (AFMC) and responsible for the development, acquisition, testing, deployment and sustainment of all air-delivered weapons. The 46th Test Wing is part of the AAC and is the command authority for the 40th Flight Test Squadron (FLTS), which flies a diverse selection of aircraft including F-15C/D Eagles, F-15E Strike Eagles, F-16A/B/C/D Fighting Falcons and the newly-upgraded A-10C Thunderbolt to meet the wing mission objectives. The men and women of the 40th are test experts, with most being Edwards' Test Pilot School graduates. Lt Col Glenn Graham was the commander of the 40th FLTS in September 2005: 'I oversee all aspects of personnel manning, business planning, and operations execution for what is the most diverse flight test squadron in the

Top: **Home of USAF testing on the East coast, a 40th FLTS F-16B flies over the Eglin test flightlines.** *Jamie Hunter/AVIACOM*

Left: **Breaking for the camera, Lockheed Martin F-16B of the 40th FLTS, callsign 'Python 1', pulls hard over the Gulf range near Eglin.** *Jamie Hunter/AVIACOM*

USAF. There will always be a place for "seat-of-the-pants" test flying, but the rigorous planning and preparation that goes into flights these days, compared to sorties in the early days of flight test, makes testing far less risky to both the programs and the aircrews. Today, we have much better models to assess what we think will happen on a given test before we go and fly it. Additionally, through modern simulation and better risk mitigation processes and when our aircrews go out to fly a mission, whether it be a weapons separation sortie, flutter analysis mission or a software upgrade flight, our crews have a much better idea of what the results will be and what will be required to achieve those results than their predecessors had back in the 1960s.

'Our recent flutter and loads testing on FMS (Foreign Military Sales) F-16s was very expensive testing that required very complex test instrumentation to measure aeroelastic characteristics and structural loadings of a given airframe for various configurations. Because FMS F-16 variants are slightly different to USAF airframes, if our test aircraft breaks (or components on the aircraft) we've incurred some program delays because these aircraft are unique. However, we've been able to overcome these problems by working with the contractors and our instrumentation experts to give high priority to fixing these assets. There is little doubt that simulators will become more and more advanced, but you will still need to go out and do the testing in a real airplane in the sky. What is nice is that we still get some classic flight test programs. A highlight for me recently was the opportunity to conduct a complete flight test on the new Coast Guard RU-38 reconnaissance aircraft. There were only a handful of pilots in the program and we did virtually every type of testing that is taught at test pilot school on that airplane.'

Opposite, clockwise starting top left: **This F-16B is one of the aircraft built for the Pakistan Air Force but never delivered due to an arms embargo in the 1990s. The aircraft sat for many years in storage at AMARC before being delivered to the USAF test community, as well as to the US Navy as adversary aircraft.** *Jamie Hunter/AVIACOM*

Firing, firing, now! An 'ET' F-15D fires an AIM-120 AMRAAM from the wing stub pylon. Much of the USAF's missile testing is conducted from Eglin. *USAF/Air Armament Center*

Air Armament Center in action – an F-16CG of the 40th FLTS 'pickles off' a JDAM test round over the Eglin test ranges. *USAF/Air Armament Center*

Photographed against a typically idyllic beach backdrop, a 40th FLTS F-16B heads into the pattern at Eglin. *Jamie Hunter/AVIACOM*

The 40th FLTS conducts development test for the A-10. This 'Warthog' is firing an AGM-65 Maverick. *USAF/Air Armament Center*

Joint Helmet-Mounted Cueing System (JHMCS) and the super-agile AIM-9X advanced Sidewinder close-range air-to-air missile. Capt Doug 'Happy' Seymour is the Chief F-16 pilot at the 40th: 'We are tasked primarily to conduct weapons testing and are responsible for the development test and evaluation of all conventional weapons entering the USAF inventory. That being said, we conduct a wide variety of ground and airborne testing as well. Our F-15 flight is responsible for testing new flight software OFPs (operational flight programs) for all USAF F-15A to D, F-15Es and A-10 Thunderbolts

CUTTING EDGE

All new equipment, no matter how small, is tested to exhaustion in the 'Development Test' phase by either the 40th here at Eglin, or across at Edwards. The biggest current program for the USAF Lockheed Martin F-16 Fighting Falcon force is the immense Common Configuration Implementation Program (CCIP) currently introducing common hardware and software capability to 650 Block 40/42/50/52 'Vipers'. Improvements include colour cockpit displays, datalink, the amazing

The author in the cockpit with the testers of the 40th FLTS on an F-16 mission from Eglin. *Jamie Hunter/AVIACOM*

and the majority of our testing involves load compatibility flight profile testing and safe weapons separation testing. The load compatibility portion looks at whether or not the aircraft will have any structural problems while carrying the new test item and our flutter testing investigates any aeroelastic issues of the aircraft that are generated by the test item. The compatibility flight profile is conducted to ensure that the test item will not be damaged by the flight regime in which it will be operated. During safe separation testing we make sure the test item will not damage the aircraft during release, and also that it will perform as required after release. And of course during all testing we are going to assess how the item affects the aircraft's handling qualities. Other testing that we have conducted lately include items such as JHMCS and new panoramic night-vision goggles. We also support a lot of other testing by pro-

viding chase aircraft for programs such as F-22A Raptor as well as Trident and Tomahawk cruise missiles. We are going to be testing the new R7 pod for the F-16 here shortly and will be checking to make sure that it is able to withstand manoeuvres that it will be put through during flight. This will include wind-up turns (symmetric, positive-G manoeuvres), balanced steady push-overs (symmetric, negative-G manoeuvres), loaded rolls and negative-G load rolls and will be conducted out to the flight clearance limits for the pod. Additionally, the pilot will be assessing the effects of carrying the pod with respect to the aircraft handling qualities.'

With all F-15 Eagle testing having ceased at Edwards, the two Eglin test units (40th FLTS and the 85th TES) as well as the 422nd TES at Nellis now handle all flight test work for the type. The Suite 5E upgrade for the F-15E mainly involves expanding Strike Eagle capabilities to carry GPS-guided weapons on more stations. The F-15E is also carrying the incredibly accurate Sniper pod and is also the lead integration platform for Boeing's 250 lb Small Diameter Bomb (SDB).

Right: **The 40th FLTS F-15E Strike Eagles are at the forward edge of development for the type. The squadron's aircrews and maintenance personnel work hard to get the latest hardware and software tested and ready for the front line.** *Jamie Hunter/AVIACOM*

In August 2004, a 40th FLTS F-15E dropped the first GBU-39 SDB on a test mission from Eglin as the squadron got flight testing under way ahead of IOC (Initial Operating Capability) planned for 2006.

As well as conducting the majority of F-15E development testing, the squadron fulfils a similar role for the A-10 Thunderbolt II. The 'Warthog', as it is affectionately known, is a type constantly in the spotlight and it continues to prove its worth. The 40th FLTS is at the centre of a program to enhance the 'Hog's capabilities in its primary Close Air Support (CAS) role, adding a precision strike capability.

Cruising into initials at Eglin, 'Python 1' flies over Choctawhatchee Bay's Highway 293 bridge, near the beach resort of Destin. *Jamie Hunter/AVIACOM*

The Precision Engagement System (PES) will give the upgraded A-10C a new digital stores management system, new cockpit displays and a Situation Awareness Data Link (SADL). The integration of the Joint Direct Attack Munition (JDAM) and Wind Corrected Munitions Dispenser (WCMD) is planned, along with the introduction

Left: **Going ballistic! 'Python 1', an F-16B operated by the 40th FLTS, goes into the vertical. The squadron's F-16s are used extensively for chase duties.** *Jamie Hunter/AVIACOM*

Below left: **A fine study of a 40th FLTS 'Viper' high above Eglin. The squadron's F-16Bs are used extensively for chase and proficiency missions.** *Jamie Hunter/AVIACOM*

Right: **The F-16 is by far the most numerous aircraft type operated by the 40th FLTS. This F-16B is seen on a mission from Eglin in September 2005 over the Gulf test range complex to the south of the base.** *Jamie Hunter/AVIACOM*

of the popular Lockheed Martin Sniper pod. The 40th has also been evaluating a new variant of the Raytheon AGM-65 Maverick air-to-ground missile. The new variant will boast four times the range of current versions and will give pilots the ability to target the weapon using GPS co-ordinates rather than the current visual lock. The Maverick Lock-on-After-Launch (LOAL) involves fitting a GPS receiver and datalink to the missile. This interfaces with a datalink in the LAU-117 launch rail. Pilots will also be able to use datalinked target imagery or pass control of the missile to other similarly configured aircraft. A further proposal is for an extended range Maverick with a booster engine to enable it to hit targets at greater stand-off ranges of up to 100 miles. A structural upgrade and new TF34-100B improved thrust engines are also planned, and coupled with possible re-winging, could see the A-10 through to as far as the year 2028.

Above: **A Block 50 F-16D of the 40th FLTS during testing of GBU-15 bombs in the EDGE weapons test program. EDGE (Exploitation of DGPS for Guidance Enhancement) used Differential GPS (DGPS) targeting updates datalinked to the F-16 from a ground station.** *USAF/Air Armament Center*

Right: **An F-16A from the 40th FLTS carrying an AGM-65 Maverick prepares to refuel from a KC-135R.** *USAF/SSgt Jerry Morrison*

Left: **Test dropping an AGM-158 JASSM (Joint Air-to-Surface Stand-off Missile) cruise missile. JASSM faced termination from Congress having failed two FOT&E trials, however thanks to 53rd Wing trials the weapon has matured and is now extremely effective.**
USAF/Air Armament Center

Below: **Short finals – F-16B callsign 'Python 01' coming in to land at Eglin over the shores of Choctawhatchee Bay.**
Jamie Hunter/AVIACOM

Above: **The 40th FLTS conducts the majority of development testing for the F-15E Strike Eagle. The Small Diameter Bomb (SDB) is a major program for the squadron, having conducted a number of test drops of the Boeing 250 lb GBU-39 precision-guided weapon during the 36-month System Development and Demonstration (SDD) phase that began in October 2003. The weapon's small size will allow it to be carried on almost all weapons platforms including F-15E, F-22A, F-35 Joint Strike Fighter and the Joint Unmanned Combat Air System (J-UCAS).**
Jamie Hunter/AVIACOM

Right: **On the flightline at Eglin, an F-15D of the 40th FLTS awaits its test aircrew for a mission.** *Jamie Hunter/AVIACOM*

Above: **The GBU-15 is based on the 2,000 lb Mk 84 general-purpose (GP) bomb or BLU-109 penetrating warhead. The weapon can attack using the direct attack mode, which means the pilot locks the weapon onto the target and the weapon guides itself to the target, or the indirect attack mode where the WSO actively guides the bomb via the AXQ-14 datalink pod to the selected target. The EGBU-15 seen here adds GPS/INS guidance to achieve all-weather capability and improved accuracy.** *USAF*

Inset: **The first upgraded A-10C on its maiden flight from Eglin on 20 January 2005.** *USAF*

Left: **The cockpit of the A-10C features new multi-function displays and a new head-up display (HUD).** *Kevin Jackson*

Above: **On finals to Eglin following a test mission, the 40th FLTS A-10C is part of an accelerated integrated test program alongside the 422nd TES at Nellis. Note the red test equipment fits on the aircraft and the large instrumentation pitot on the nose.** *USAF*

Nutcrackers

The 413th Flight Test Squadron at Hurlburt Field is part of Eglin's 46th Test Wing and it is responsible for Developmental Test and Evaluation of Air Force Special Operations Command (AFSOC) platforms such as the MC-130 Hercules, AC-130 Hercules gunship, MH-53 Pave Low and HH-60G. The 413th is co-located with the 18th FLTS which is also at Hurlburt. Aircrews here are attached to the operational AFSOC squadrons at the base and use AFSOC aircraft as required. Detachment 1 of the 413th is at Nellis AFB and is responsible for developmental testing of the HH-60G Pave Hawk. As an integral member of the HH-60 Combined Test Force (CTF), Det 1 in partnership with Detachment 3, 18 FLTS, provides the full range of DT/OT to support AFSOC's Combat Search and Rescue (CSAR) mission.

The 40th FLTS operates this NC-130H Hercules. Sister special operations test unit 413th FLTS was previously a detachment of the 40th FLTS at Hurlburt Field. *Jamie Hunter/AVIACOM*

Jamie Hunter/AVIACOM

A trio of 85th TES ('OT') Block 50 F-16s, led by Lt Col J Todd Hicks, seen on a test mission from Eglin. The nearest aircraft, an F-16D, carries a pair of AIM-9X, with all pilots wearing the Joint Helmet- Mounted Cueing System (JHMCS). *Jamie Hunter/AVIACOM*

53RD WING

Sharpening the Sword

Whether it's F-22A Raptors developing tactics to command the skies, F-15Es dropping new bombs, F-16s developing latest radar killing techniques, B-2s attacking silently in the night or QF-4 Phantoms flying unmanned missions as targets – there is one wing in the USAF that does it all. Alongside the 40th FLTS, the realistic operational testing (OT) is the realm of the 53rd Wing, also headquartered at Eglin. This wing serves as a focal point for tactical aircraft evaluation ahead of service clearance and flies an incredibly diverse mission with a wide variety of aircraft. The wing's operational test flying activities are split between a number of bases in the US, with small detachments at Holloman AFB supporting the F-117A, at Dyess for the B-1B, at Barksdale for the B-52H and at Whiteman for the B-2A. However, it is in two particular regions that the wing has truly stamped its mark – the golden sandy beaches of the Florida Panhandle on the Gulf Coast and the rugged desert of the gambler's home of Las Vegas in Nevada. The Florida home of the 53rd Wing is at Eglin AFB, near Fort Walton Beach, a dream posting in a wonderful location. Down the coast at Panama City, Tyndall AFB is

Lt Col J Todd Hicks, commander of the 85th TES at the controls of 'Racer 1', heading back to Eglin from the Gulf range following an exhausting 2v2 BFM test mission. *Jamie Hunter/AVIACOM*

TESTING TOP GUNS | 53

Above: **85th TES 'Skulls' F-16C/Ds break away from the camera over the Gulf test range near Eglin.** *Jamie Hunter/AVIACOM*

Right: **'Racers in place 90 right'. Two 85th TES F-16CJs set up for some 2v2 air combat out over the Gulf test range near Eglin. The squadron conducts operational test and evaluation of new equipment for the F-15 and F-16.** *Jamie Hunter/AVIACOM*

another outpost for the wing while, across in Nevada, the gambling takes a back seat for the testers at Nellis AFB.

Two of the most prominent squadrons within the 53rd Wing are the 85th Test and Evaluation Squadron (TES) Eglin and the 422nd TES at Nellis. Lt Col J Todd Hicks commands the 85th TES 'Skulls' at Eglin in 2005, 'I have been flying the F-16 since 1988 and I have 2,700hrs of flight time in the F-16. I have been in operational test for four years. My current job as commander of the 85th TES sees me conducting operational testing on all new software, hardware, weaponry for the F-16.' The USAF is working hard to streamline its development test and operational test activities as it seeks to react swiftly to operational requirements and get new products to the front line as quickly and efficiently as possible. New systems have traditionally first been sent for DT with the Combined Test Forces (CTFs) Edwards AFB, CA, or with the Air Armament Center here at Eglin, however, now the operational test community of the 53rd Wing is getting involved with programs much earlier now'. Lt Col Hicks continued, 'There is a big merging of DT and OT going on now. We are

streamlining the process and trying to shorten the time line (and reduce costs). In the past, the 40th FLTS and the 416th (F-16 CTF at Edwards) would do a complete DT and hand us a product that was pretty true and tried. Then we would take that product and we'd conduct operational testing on it. Now, they can do one safety of flight test and then they give it to both of us for combined testing.'

Lt Col Sam 'Boomer' Shaneyfelt is the operations officer with the 85th TES: 'Essentially, the 40th FLTS next door does all the initial bed-down for software and some of the hardware development for almost everything that is fielded on the F-16'. They say, 'Did the contractor meet specification for what the USAF required or any other FMS foreign sales, in a simple manner and in a very controlled environment does the thing work as advertised? We take what they've done and say can we fight with it? So we take the equipment and we go against adversaries or against surface-to-air and air-to-air threats and we'll fight our way through and come back and make a recommendation on whether we should field this or not.'

The 'Skulls' are heavily involved with the biggest upgrade the USAF has ever undertaken for the F-16. The Common Configuration Implementation Program (CCIP) essentially brings the Block 40 and Block 50 F-16C/Ds to a common standard. However, the SAM-killing Block 50/52 F-16CJ will retain the edge as it becomes a true multi-role platform. In 2005 the 'Skulls' completed operational testing of the M4.2+ core avionics suite to permit joint carriage of the Sniper Advanced Targeting Pod (ATP) and the CJ's ASQ-213 HARM Targeting System (HTS). Lt Col Hicks commented, 'This is the F-16 we've been waiting for. It's been an evolution of more than 20 years to be able to execute all tactical combat missions ranging from

Below: **The busy test flightline at Eglin. The F-16CJ in the foreground carries the new Lockheed Martin Sniper advanced targeting pod. This new pod not only radically improves ground targeting but is also a tool for positively identifying both ground and aerial targets.** *Jamie Hunter/AVIACOM*

Left: **Looks can kill – experienced F-16 pilot Lt Col David Lujan, commander of the 86th FWS, at the controls of an 85th TES F-16DJ wearing the JHMCS (Joint Helmet-Mounted Cueing System). This highly accurate cueing system provides pilots with 'First look, First shot' high off-boresight weapons engagement capabilities. JHMCS enables the pilot to accurately direct and cue weapons and sensors against aerial and ground targets whilst performing high-G manoeuvres.** *Jamie Hunter/AVIACOM*

Above: **Lt Col J Todd Hicks, 85th TES commander, leads a flight of Eglin and Edwards F-16s during combined developmental and operational testing of the M4.2+ avionics suite for the Block 50/52 variant that permits dual carriage of the Sniper Advanced Targeting Pod (ATP) and the ASQ-213 HARM Targeting System (HTS).** *USAF/Tom Reynolds*

Left: **The view from the back seat of an 85th TES F-16D during a mission from Eglin in September 2005.** *Jamie Hunter/AVIACOM*

Below: **The 85th TES and its associated units are heavily involved with operationally testing new weapons. This view from the back seat of an F-16D shows an AGM-88 High Speed Anti Radiation Missile (HARM) being fired over the test range. The HARM is an air-to-surface missile designed to seek and destroy enemy radar-equipped air defence systems.** *USAF/TSgt Michael Ammons*

The new Raytheon HARM HDAM (HARM Destruction of Enemy Air Defence Attack Module) program started in 2005 and is an update for the current standard missile. The USAF is pursuing this project rather than following the US Navy's AGM-88E AARGM (Advanced Anti-Radiation Guided Missile). The HDAM is being run in parallel with the development and operational testing of an upgraded version of the ASQ-213 HARM Targeting System (HTS) pod. Designated the R7 STING (Smart Targeting and Identification via Networked Geolocation), development testing is being conducted by the 416th FLTS at Edwards, with flight suitability testing by the 40th FLTS at Eglin with the R7 on both the right and left chin station, and also on the left chin while carrying a Sniper pod on the right chin. Expected to enter service in September 2006, the R7 STING will allow the HTS to be cued by offboard sensors, allowing more precise launch. *USAF/TSgt Michael Ammons*

precision engagement to suppression of enemy air defences to air superiority. When I first started flying the F-16 we had free-falling munitions and limited air-to-air capability. It's been an evolution of more than 20 years to be able to execute all tactical combat missions ranging from precision engagement to suppression of enemy air defences to air superiority'.

The 85th shares its F-16 test work with its sister squadron across at Nellis, the 422nd TES 'Green Bats'. The workloads between the two squadrons are carefully planned, but essentially the Nellis 'Viper' team handles Block 40/42 work, the 'Skulls' look after the Block 50/52. As well as its F-16s, the squadron also support the 40th FLTS with operational testing of the F-15C/D Eagle and the F-15E Strike Eagle, which is also conducted by the 'Green Bats' but in the Nellis environs. It is clear that the mission of the 'Skulls' at Eglin places huge demands on the personnel and aircraft, working in the most incredible of environments and it is difficult to portray the stresses and strains that come with this job. Lt Col Hicks described a recent high-pressure mission: 'I recently flew a dress rehearsal for an upcoming live air-to-air missile shot. A dress rehearsal is when all players simulate launching a live missile in order to uncover any potential problem areas that could be

Centre right: **Skull Section – a trio of 85th TES 'OT' F-15C, F-15E and F-16C over typical Florida scenery near Eglin.** *USAF*

Right: **Flying over Destin, near Eglin, an F-15C of the 85th TES heads out to the range for a basic fighter manoeuvres (BFM) training mission.** *USAF/TSgt Michael Ammons*

An F-15E Strike Eagle armed with a live AIM-120 AMRAAM from the 85th TES's sister unit, the 422nd TES, flies over the beach near Eglin whilst deployed from Nellis. *USAF/TSgt Michael Ammons*

encountered during the live launch. For this particular mission there was a full-scale QF-4 drone flying the planned profile. Ground Control Intercept (GCI) assisted myself and the QF-4 into launch parameters where I simulated launching the missile. The dress rehearsal was a success and we're ready to fire the live missile.'

Wing Roots

The 53rd Wing traces its roots back to 1961 when the US Army set out to take the close air support (CAS) and tactical airlift missions away from the USAF. On 16 September 1963 Tactical Air Command (TAC) formed the 4475th Tactical Air Warfare Group at Eglin to plan joint Army and USAF testing, later becoming the Tactical Air

Above: **Lt Col Anthony Murphy, commander of the 85th TES in 2004, prepares for a sortie in an F-15C (callsign 'Mozam 01'). He wears the Joint Helmet-Mounted Cueing System (JHMCS) and the Eagle is carrying the latest AIM-9X Sidewinder air-to-air missile. The helmet and missile have been integrated under HOBS – High Off-Boresight Seeker. This allows the pilot to cue the missile through the visor display.** *Jamie Hunter/AVIACOM*

Right: **Maj Michael Hoepfner of the 85th TES at Eglin AFB releases a CBU-103 Wind Corrected Munitions Dispensor (WCMD) from his F-16CJ over the Nellis range complex during tests for the 28th Test Squadron, also from Eglin.** *USAF MSgt Michael Ammons*

Warfare Center (TAWC) with the remit of improving tactical aviation in support of ground troops.

In Vietnam, the wing led the way with some inspirational programs such as 'Pave Nail', a program to find and destroy targets with precision. This was the start of the precision warfare we see today and consisted of a podded system aboard an OV-10 Bronco with a navigational radio and a laser designator to illuminate targets for laser-guided bombs (LGBs). By 1972 the TAWC was heavily involved in developmental testing and evaluation, as well as operational testing and evaluation and was becoming an important node for the USAF. The addition of the air-to-air weapons system evaluation program (WSEP) marked the start of its role in evaluating fielded combat

'We sharpen the sword, and strengthen the shield'

The USAF 53rd Wing is comprised of the following:

53rd Weapons Evaluation Group (WEG)

Located at Tyndall AFB, FL, and composed of five squadrons and two detachments: 53rd Test Support Squadron, 81st Range Control Squadron, 82nd Aerial Targets Squadron (ATRS), 83rd Fighter Weapons Squadron (FWS) at Tyndall and the 86th FWS at Eglin, while Det 1 of the 82nd ATRS is at Holloman AFB, NM, and Det 1 of the 86th FWS is at Hill AFB, UT. The WEG is responsible for the Air-to-Air Weapon System Evaluation Program (WSEP), also known as 'Combat Archer'. It is also responsible for the Air-to-Ground WSEP – 'Combat Hammer'. It also provides aerial targets in the shape of QF-4 Phantoms and smaller drones for the Gulf Ranges and the White Sands Missile Range in New Mexico.

53rd Test and Evaluation Group (TEG)

This group comprises numerous squadrons at 17 US bases including the 85th Test and Evaluation Squadron (TES) at Eglin, the 31st TES at Edwards, the 422nd TES at Nellis, the 72nd TES at Whiteman, the 337th TES at Dyess, the Air National Guard/Air Force Reserve Test Center at Tuscon and the 49th TS at Barksdale, not to mention detachments at bases such as Holloman and Luke. The TEG manages all wing flying activities as it executes operational test and evaluation, tactics development, and evaluation projects handed to it from Air Combat Command (ACC). The 59th TES at Nellis is part of the 53rd Test and Management Group and manages Force Development Evaluations (FDE) and Tactics Development and Evaluations (TD&E) of the F-22A's weaponry and avionics, as well as the FDE and TD&E for F-15C/D, F-15E, F-16, and the A-10.

53rd Test Management Group (TMG)

Located at Eglin AFB, this group primarily provides oversight for planning and management of testing performed by the 53rd TEG, 53rd EWG and 53 WEG. The 53rd TMG is comprised of five units: the 53rd Computer Systems Squadron (CSS), 28th Test Squadron, 29th Training Systems Squadron (TSS), the 59th Test and Evaluation Squadron, and the Operational Flight Program Combined Test Force (OFP CTF).

Above: **'Skulls' F-16s head into the sunset on a typically beautiful Gulf Coast afternoon. The picturesque area around Eglin suffers from some severe weather as well as its usual idyllic conditions.** *Jamie Hunter/AVIACOM*

Right: **Lt Col Hicks leads fellow F-16 colleagues from the operational test and evaluation squadron 85th TES 'Skulls'.** *Jamie Hunter/AVIACOM*

Above: **Late afternoon light catches 'OT' F-16s of the 85th TES heading into the break at Eglin following a mission.**
Jamie Hunter/AVIACOM

Right: **Lt Col J Todd Hicks and Lt Col David Lujan pose in front of an 85th TES F-16CJ following a mission from Eglin.**
Jamie Hunter/AVIACOM

capabilities to determine effectiveness as well as to increased its emphasis on aircrew training. When Red Flag exercises started it was the result of realisation that most combat losses occurred during a pilot's first eight to ten missions. TAWC took on sister exercise Blue Flag, to train battle staff and increase cohesion between the commander, planners, and the forces under their control.

On 1 October 1991 the Tactical Air Warfare Center was redesignated as the Air Warfare Center, later being reassigned to the newly formed Air Combat Command and it moved to the principle of one base; one boss; one command. By October 1995, the USAF consolidated the AWC with the inactive 53rd FW, and the 53rd Wing was born.

Right: **On the line at Eglin, a 'Skulls' F-16CJ is prepared for a mission.** *Jamie Hunter/AVIACOM*

Below right: **The Block 50 F-16C/D is powered by the General Electric F110-GE-129 engine. This example also carries a pair of Raytheon AIM-9X advanced Sidewinders.** *Jamie Hunter/AVIACOM*

WEAPONS SPECIALIST

Lt Col David 'Loogie' Lujan is the commander of the 86th Fighter Weapons Squadron (FWS), part of the 53rd Wing and the weapons evaluation group (WEG) based at Eglin: 'We evaluate performance of fielded and to-be-fielded precision munitions. If it exists, we evaluate it. We have a flavour of everything on the squadron, we have F-16 pilots, F-117 guys, F-15 guys – I have personally flown F-16s for 19 years and have 3,500 hours. I was an instructor at the weapons school at Nellis and now my role as commander is to lead my team to accomplish the air-to-ground Weapons System Evaluation Program (WSEP) or "Combat Hammer" as the program is also called. We basically give the USAF leadership an accurate expectation of precision-guided weapon performance. We are the only organisation in the USAF that employs all our PGMs in an operationally representative way and reverse-engineers the effects. Pretty soon "Combat Hammer" will be the only place that USAF aircrews can employ large-footprint weapons like JSOW, JASSM and SDB in peacetime. We have a detachment at Hill AFB since we deploy to Hill to do most of our work. There is simply is no substitute to building, loading, employing and analyzing the real thing. I was recently in an F-16 chasing a B-2 dropping an enormous GPS weapon. The B-2 was at 45,000ft and very slow. The most challenging part was staying with the bomber at that altitude; the B-2 simply has no perspective and silhouette due to its shape, so it is tricky to fly chase on this beast. After he dropped we chased the weapon all the way until it impacted on the Utah Test and Training Range (UTTR).'

Dragon's Lair

Across at Holloman AFB, NM, the 53rd Test and Evaluation Group Detachment 1 plays an important role in the operational testing for the Lockheed Martin F-117A Nighthawk. In 2003 it operated 'The Dragon', a grey-painted F-117 that was engaged in trials to determine whether the type could have a role in daytime combat operations. Lt Col Kevin Sullivan was the 53rd TEG Det 1 commander at the time and he commented that the aircraft was flying up to two missions per day for its trials. Lt Col Buck Rogers, Det 1 operations officer (OPSO) said, 'The Chief of Staff wants to have a 24-hour stealth presence over future battlefields. We know our current black paint scheme wouldn't be a good colour for daytime operations'. Maj Tre Urso said, 'We use the F-117 for everything from new tactics development to the evaluation of new software or hardware. Det 1 has been involved in all the F-117 modifications and upgrades over the years. This trial provides a great opportunity for us to learn about our daytime capabilities and limitations. It also helps us evaluate how the new paints will hold up over time and lets us measure the impact the colour modification has on the maintenance troops who maintain the jet. Bottom line, we need to make sure we provide our leaders an accurate assessment of the costs and benefits involved with daytime ops and the gray paint scheme.'

In the 'Canyon' at Holloman, 'The Dragon' was a grey-painted F-117A of Det 1, 53rd TEG, used for operational testing of the type. *Jamie Hunter/AVIACOM*

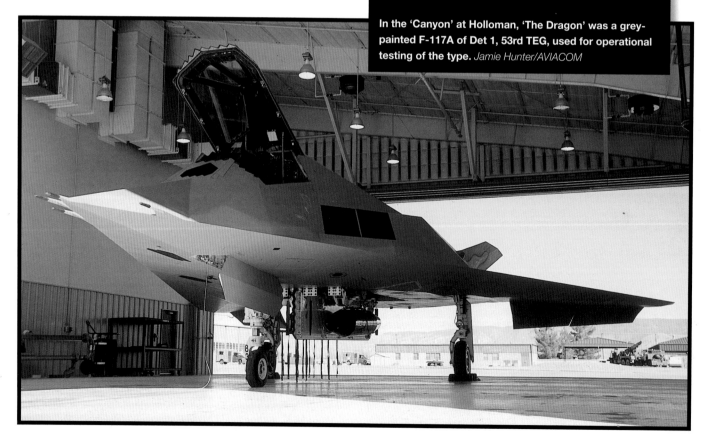

RHINO FLIGHT

The 82nd Aerial Targets Squadron (ATRS) at Tyndall is the last unit in the US operating the mighty McDonnell Douglas F-4 Phantom, albeit as Full Scale Aerial Target (FSAT) QF-4 standard for important test duties, along with its Det 1 at Holloman led by Lt Col Charlie 'Tuna' Hainline. These are the last operational Phantoms in the US, the last front line F-4Gs having been retired back in 1996. The 82nd ATRS can usually count on having around 45 converted QF-4 Phantoms on strength, although only a handful are on the flightline for manned missions at any given time and most are rotated in and out of maintenance and storage. A further batch is earmarked for termination and is therefore readied for unmanned missions.

The 82nd ATRS 'Team Target' is part of the 53rd WEG and is heavily involved with 'Combat Archer' and provides all USAF aerial target support for the Gulf Ranges near Eglin and White Sands Missile Range near Holloman. Around 90% the Phantom missions here are flown manned by the Lockheed Martin contractor and USAF pilots for missile and radar testing out over the Gulf Ranges. The small cadre of F-4 pilots are kept busy flying manned dress rehearsal manoeuvre profiles for the local test units, from relatively benign to full-up 'turning and burning' as the missile envelope is expanded to track the F-4. This inevitably ends up with an unmanned F-4 mission and a live missile shot. For the unmanned (or NULLO – Not Under Live Local Operator) missions, the QF-4s use the 'Drone Way' at Tyndall, a secluded runway to the south of the main base, specifically earmarked for QF-4 operations. The squadron also operates a pair of E-9A 'Widget' sea surveillance aircraft (based on the DHC-8 Dash 8) to sweep the ranges and plot ship positions in the range. It also employs the BQM-134 sub-scale drone and the soon-to-be-retired MQM-107 drone and is the only USAF squadron to have boats on strength, these being used to head out into the Gulf and retrieve the sub-scale drones if they are downed.

Under the command of Lt Col Jerry 'Jive' Kerby in 2005, the 82nd ATRS has been busy supporting the USAF 'Heritage Flight' at airshows around the US with its six immaculate QF-4Es painted in camouflage schemes to represent four decades of USAF F-4 operations. Lt Col Kerby said, 'We are here to honour the men and women that flew and worked on this airplane. That's why we have done these commemorative paint jobs, so they can see them back in the air again, to bring them back to how they looked when they worked on them. Everybody comes by and tells you stories. They either worked on them or flew them. The F-4 is so popular, and there is a lot of pride in the jet'.

The 82nd ATRS 'Team Target' operates the QF-4 Phantom from Tyndall AFB, near Panama City in Florida. The squadron supports a number of test missions and has in recent years painted six of its QF-4Es in special camouflage schemes to represent the operational life of the F-4 in USAF service. Seen here over Panama City beach, Lt Col Jerry Kerby leads a section of two 'Heritage' QF-4Es heading out from Tyndall. *Jamie Hunter/AVIACOM*

Left: **The QF-4s of the 82nd ATRS fly mission profiles to test new missiles. The aircraft can also be flown unmanned for live shots to ultimately test the lethality of new weapons.** *Jamie Hunter/AVIACOM*

Below: **Wearing its immaculate South-East Asia livery of sand, two-tone green and light grey underside, QF-4E 72-1490 carries the standard 'TD' tailcode of the 82nd ATRS as well as the original black and white check fin band of the 82nd Fighter Squadron. The aircraft is flown here by Lt Col Jerry 'Jive' Kerby, leading Lt Col Anthony 'ET' Murphy in 'Rhino 2'. Lt Col Murphy was the deputy commander of the 53rd WEG in 2005.** *Jamie Hunter/AVIACOM*

Right: **Cruising above Tyndall, an 82nd ATRS QF-4E in heritage 'Egypt One' colours.** *Jamie Hunter/AVIACOM*

Below right: **Lt Col Kerby in the cockpit of the 'European One' camouflaged QF-4E following a mission from Tyndall in September 2005.** *Jamie Hunter/AVIACOM*

Bottom right: **On the 82nd ATRS flightline at Tyndall as two 'Heritage' QF-4Es return from a mission over the Gulf ranges. The grey and red QF-4E in the background wears the standard QF-4 operational scheme. These cherished jets are kept in first class working order by the dedicated Lockheed Martin contractor ground technicians.** *Jamie Hunter/AVIACOM*

Above: **The 'Egypt One' two-tone grey QF-4E (74-1652), flown here by experienced Lockheed Martin pilot Sal Bonacasa, last served with the 35th TFW at George AFB, CA.** *Jamie Hunter/AVIACOM*

Left: **A pair of QF-4Es head back to Tyndall over the long silver strand beaches of Florida.** *Jamie Hunter/AVIACOM*

Below left: **'Rhino break' – immaculate 'Heritage' QF-4Es of the 82nd ATRS (radio callsign 'Rhino').** *Jamie Hunter/AVIACOM*

INTO THE FUTURE

It is clear from the number of programs running for the USAF's fighter-bomber fleet that the test teams at Eglin and its sister bases are going to remain as busy as ever. The constant stream of programs and updates has seen the need to promote greater understanding, not only between development test and operational test units, but also between platforms and commands. Indeed, plans are afoot to hold a 'Test Flag' at Nellis AFB, NV, from 2005 to specifically develop tactics and understanding to underpin the technology. This major exercise could be designed to develop time-sensitive targeting (TST) and Suppression of Enemy Air Defence (SEAD) tactics, enhance CAOC (Combined Air Operations Centre) functionality and decrease sensor-to-shooter time through greater use of datalinks and other communications methods to get decisions from command centres. The testers at Eglin are leading the way for the front line squadrons, taking innovation from its early steps and making it a workable and efficient asset for the warfighter.

Chapter Three
Nellis Warriors

Home of the 'Green Bats'

What is the biggest thrill you can get in Las Vegas. A winning hand at the Blackjack table, a ride on 'Big Shot' on the Stratosphere hotel tower, a flight over the Grand Canyon? How about flying in the world's most advanced superfighter? For pilots of the 422nd Test and Evaluation Squadron (TES) at Nellis AFB the latter is an everyday event. Nellis has long been dubbed 'Home of the fighter pilot', and with good reason. This massive base with its associated ranges in the desolate desert to the north of Las Vegas plays host to the massive 'Red Flag' exercises. Aircrew and support teams come here to learn how to use their aircraft in anger in realistic combat scenarios. The 422nd TES 'Green Bats' is part of the 53rd Wing and a sister squadron to the 85th TES 'Skulls' at Eglin and is responsible for a diverse range of operational test and evaluation from Nellis.

On a daily basis, the 422nd TES launches waves of missions amongst the busy Red Flag schedule to push new equipment to the limits over the Nellis range complex and see if it is suitable for pilots out on the front line. Commander Lt Col Jeff Weed explained, 'We have the biggest fighter squadron in ACC here with five aircraft types (A-10, F-15C/E, F-16 and F-22A) and 70 aircrew, most of whom are Weapons School graduates here at Nellis. We are here to innovate, to test and to teach – the capabilities we have here can be as much as five years ahead of the field. Our work involves analyzing what will and what won't work; we try new tactics and try different approaches to things, flying realistic missions with the new piece of equipment here at Nellis. We act as the finishing-line chequered flag for new

'Green Bats' in action. A pair of F-22A Raptors lead an F-15E of the 422nd TES during a mission from Nellis. *Katsuhiko Tokunaga*

products, when we are finished with it it goes out to the front line. We also head out to squadrons and teach skills with the new systems, in fact we recently went to Lakenheath to teach the 48th FW about a new radar modification for the F-15E. We work closely with the co-located 59th TES (part of the 53rd Test and Management Group) they plan, report on and manage what we do here. From a leadership perspective this is one of the only places where all fighter types in the inventory can fly and fight with and against each other. The F-15E guys can see what F-22A Raptor can do, so we can all see what's possible. Our folks here are the best qualified to ensure we get the best "bang for the buck". We can test very quickly and respond to requirements. The GBU-38 500 lb JDAM was a good case in point. We got that weapon out to the F-15E and F-16 community in less than a month thanks to combined DT/OT'.

Left: Jamie Hunter/AVIACOM

Above: **Punching flares, an F-15E Strike Eagle dispenses decoys. The 'Green Bats' of the 422nd TES operate both F-15Es and F-15Cs for operational testing.** *Jamie Hunter/AVIACOM*

Right: **On the 422nd TES flightline at Nellis, an F-22A Raptor prepares for an operational test mission.** *Jamie Hunter/AVIACOM*

Above: **An A-10 Thunderbolt of 'Hog' flight of the 422nd TES. The squadron is engaged in combined development and operational testing for this rugged aircraft.** *Jamie Hunter/AVIACOM*

THE DARK SIDE

The most awesome hardware on the flightline at Nellis are the 422nd's Lockheed Martin F-22A Raptors. Initial Raptor deliveries to Nellis for the 'Green Bats' to commence operational testing for the type came on 14 January 2003, with this aircraft quickly joined by a further seven aircraft to develop Raptor tactics, techniques and operating procedures. The 422nd is conducting tests on every planned improvement before those improvements are fielded in the operational fleet. In late 2005 the squadron was heavily involved in the Follow-On Operational Test and Evaluation (FOT&E) and super-sonic clearance of Joint Direct Attack Munition (JDAM) for the type as the USAF geared up for Initial Operational Capability (IOC) in December 2005. The 422nd TES flew the first Follow-on Opera-tional Test and Evaluation mission on 29 August 2005, releasing a JDAM on the Utah Test and Training Range. The Air Force Opera-tional Test and Evaluation, Detachment 6, is the overall agency charged with performing the FOT&E, and it has divided testing on seven operationally representative Raptors into three areas. In one area, the Raptor will release JDAMs on the UTTR. Another evalua-tion will be live AIM-120 missile shots taken on the White Sands Missile Range. The third will be a mission-level evaluation flown on

Above: **Raptor up close and personal.** *Jamie Hunter/AVIACOM*

the Nevada Test and Training Range. During the FOT&E phase, testers are planning to shoot five missiles and release 16 JDAMs, according to Lt Col Weed. He continued, 'These missions are flown using tactics that future Raptor squadrons will take to war. The sce-narios are operationally realistic. The F-22A is a challenging pro-gram. It is an immature aircraft and we are working with the SPO at Wright-Patterson, the contractors and with ACC to ensure we meet IOC in December. It will be dual role from the outset and has a sig-nificant air-to-ground capability. The IOC software includes soft-ware for this and that step will see us taking charge of the jets from Lockheed Martin. Our maintenance teams with the 57th Mainte-nance Group have come a long way. We also have four new Raptor pilots that are training in house here – these are the top one percent of all officers'.

Any airspace, any situation

by Eric Hehs, Lockheed Martin *Code One* Magazine

'We joke about our missions against the Raptor because they can be fairly boring. We fly to the range. Die. Go to the tanker. Go back out. Die. Go back to the tanker. Go back out. Die a third time. Then we go home', said Lt Col Paul Huffman, the commander of the 64th Aggressor Squadron at Nellis, who has flown as an adversary against the F-22A more than twenty times. Huffman added, 'During Initial Operational Test and Evaluation last year, we rarely saw an F-22A, let alone got a shot at one. From our perspective, the airplane certainly performed better than expected. The F-22A is transformational, no doubt about it.'

Left: **Step time – briefed and ready for action, Raptor pilots head out from 422nd TES 'Ops' for an air combat training mission at Nellis.** *Jamie Hunter/AVIACOM*

Inset: **Someone order a taxi? Heading out in the 'Raptor taxi', 422nd TES F-22A pilots head for the sweltering flightline at Nellis.** *Jamie Hunter/AVIACOM*

Below: **Sunshelters give groundcrews some respite from the searing temperatures that are associated with Nellis.** *Jamie Hunter/AVIACOM*

Jamie Hunter/AVIACOM

The 64th flew almost 300 sorties against F-22A operational test pilots of the 31st Test and Evaluation Squadron (TES) based at Edwards AFB during IOT&E in 2004. 'We never got to a merge against a single F-22A during IOT&E', Huffman continued.

The 64th Aggressors are well known, as they provide adversary support for Red Flag and other large-scale exercises held at Nellis. Pilots of the 64th fly F-16C/Ds to replicate aircraft, weapons, and tactics employed by potential threats. 'We have the experience and knowledge and that's why the Air Force asked our unit to fly against the F-22A in IOT&E', Huffman continued.

Many of the IOT&E missions lasted more than three hours and included several engagements. Two F-22A pilots often flew against four F-16s from the 64th and Raptor pilots performed pre-strike sweeps, defensive counter-air missions, and surge operations. The sweeps involved clearing a given airspace for attacking aircraft (F-16s, F-15Es, and other bomb-carrying assets). The defensive counter-air missions involved defending a point or airfield against attacking aircraft. Surges involved producing a certain number of sorties in a prescribed period of time. Operational testing of the Raptor is continuing with the 422nd TES.

Lt Col Robert Garland, a former F-15C pilot who flies Raptors with the 422nd, provides an F-22A perspective on air-to-air combat in the Air Force's most advanced fighter: 'Six adversaries provide a good workout for two F-15C pilots, but for two Raptor pilots, defeating six adversaries is about as difficult as eating breakfast. We don't even break a sweat. The Raptor needs a lot of adversaries to create a challenge.'

Raptor pilot Maj James Vogel climbs aboard Raptor serial 99-4011, one of the eight Production Representative Test Vehicle (PRTV) F-22As. *Jamie Hunter/AVIACOM*

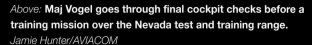

Above: **Maj Vogel goes through final cockpit checks before a training mission over the Nevada test and training range.** *Jamie Hunter/AVIACOM*

Below left: **The Raptor 'office'. The cockpit of the F-22A is dominated by four multi-function displays, with the central 'tactical display' giving the pilot an up to the minute view of the battlespace. The Raptor works on the 'dark cockpit' principle, whereby certain displays only come online to show if there is a problem.** *Katsuhiko Tokunaga*

Top right: **The groundcrew weapons specialist makes one last check of the AIM-9M Sidewinder on its extended rail before it is retracted into the internal weapons bay.** *Jamie Hunter/AVIACOM*

Below right: **The crew chief passes observation information to the pilot as the Raptor's Pratt & Whitney F119-PW-100 engines spool up. The nozzles on the engines can vector thrust 20° up or down to dramatically enhance manoeuvrability.** *Jamie Hunter/AVIACOM*

During the operational effectiveness testing portion of the F-22A IOT&E, USAF pilots flew as many as four F-22As in a variety of simulated combat scenarios. Five different F-22As were flown in the tests, which accounted for more than 500 missions and about 1,300 total flying hours. During suitability testing, the Raptor was appraised for how easily it can be deployed and maintained. The testing involved dozens of Air Force maintainers and other support personnel from Air Combat Command. Flights originated from Nellis and from Edwards AFB, California.

Lt Col Art McGettrick was commander of the 422nd TES prior to Lt Col Weed and is one of seven USAF pilots who flew the Raptor in IOT&E missions from Edwards: 'I arrived at Nellis from Edwards in October 2004 after wrapping up the IOT&E report. I can say the effectiveness tests were a resounding success overall, though details of the report are classified at a high level to protect the capabilities of the airplane. The results looked positive for suitability as well but we didn't have a chance to address all the suitability

Left: **Engines running and ready for action Maj Vogel prepares to head out for a mission from Nellis. The avionics stability of the Raptor had led to initial overheating issues in the desert heat at Nellis as software re-booting issues took time on the ground. However, software improvements have largely addressed these issues. The initial Tape 3.10 software had stability issues, however the Tape 3.12 and Tape 3.13 upgrades have dramatically improved reliability.** *Jamie Hunter/AVIACOM*

Below left: **The huge control surfaces of the Raptor are evident here as the pilot checks for full and free movement.** *Jamie Hunter/AVIACOM*

Above: **Easing out from the sunshelter, an 'OT' Raptor heads for runway 21L at Nellis.** *Jamie Hunter/AVIACOM*

Below: **A 'dry' power take-off from runway 21L, Maj James Vogel tucks the gear as he passes the famous air traffic tower at Nellis.** *Jamie Hunter/AVIACOM*

criteria since they were based on initial operational capability for the F-22A, the date the aircraft is declared ready for operational service, which is scheduled for December 2005. In other words, we could not meet criteria set for capabilities the aircraft did not yet have. We gave the Raptor a score of "effective and potentially suitable. The suitability score generated attention from officials looking for a pass or fail".'

Left: **An 'OT' Raptor bears its teeth high above the Nellis ranges, this 422nd TES F-22A opens one of its four internal weapons bays accommodating three AIM-120 AMRAAMs. The two under-fuselage bays also accommodate the two internal 1,000 lb JDAMs that can be carried and will be supplemented by the addition of the Small Diameter Bomb (SDB) to increase stand-off capability.** *Katsuhiko Tokunaga*

Centre left: **Looking for action, a 422nd TES Raptor over the Nellis ranges. Maj Alex Grynkewich of the operational test team here commented 'We haven't found an F-15 or F-16 that can find and kill us. We are flying range profiles that put a pair of Raptors up against 6-8 "aggressor" F-16Cs. We are typically ingressing at Mach 1.5 in supercruise and find we can "kill" all the F-16s in 4-5 minutes.'** *Katsuhiko Tokunaga*

Below: **The Raptor is very impressive. In late 2005 the 422nd TES and the Edwards CTF was working hard to achieve Initial Operating Capability (IOC) with the 27th FS at Langley AFB.** *Katsuhiko Tokunaga*

Right, inset: **With storm clouds building over the range, a pair of 422nd TES Raptors head back to the sanctuary of Nellis.** *Katsuhiko Tokunaga*

Right: **On finals to runway 21L, an 'OT' Raptor comes in to land over 'the desert end' at Nellis.** *Jamie Hunter/AVIACOM*

Below: **Having dealt killer blows to a flight of 'aggressor' F-16s over the range, a 422nd TES Raptor lands back at Nellis.** *Jamie Hunter/AVIACOM*

Bottom: **Taxying into the 'hot refuelling' pits at Nellis, keeping engines running and fuelling for a second mission overcomes any lack of aerial tankers and allows extended missions without having to shutdown perform maintenance procedures.** *Jamie Hunter/AVIACOM*

Top right: **Fuelled up and ready for the second 'go', a 422nd TES Raptor blasts out of Nellis past the 64th AS 'aggressor' F-16 flightline.** *Jamie Hunter/AVIACOM*

Right: **Mission accomplished. Two Nellis Raptors come into the overhead.** *Jamie Hunter/AVIACOM*

Centre right: **Sunrise break – 'OT' Raptors bathed in golden afternoon light break for landing at Nellis, framed by the famous Sunrise Mountain.** *Katsuhiko Tokunaga*

Bottom right: USAF

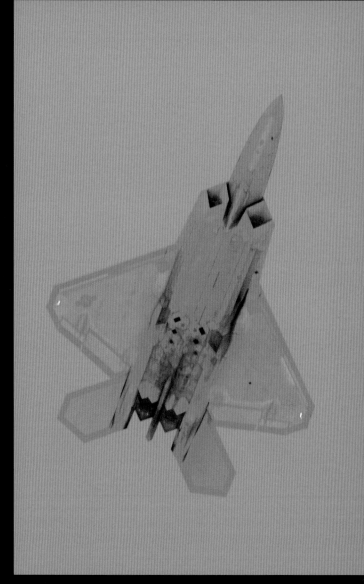

The 422nd TES also supports Red Flag exercises. Here, a 'Green Bats' F-16D formates with 64th AS 'aggressor' F-16Cs of the 'enemy' red air forces. *Richard Collens*

OUT ON THE RANGE

The 422nd TES isn't just about Raptor. This busy squadron operates five different types, as Lt Col Weed explained, 'Our A-10s are at the forward edge of the upgrade programs going on for that type. We have six permanent A-10 pilots and three attached to the unit. We currently have three upgraded A-10Cs and two more are due. They have a new cockpit and are flying with the Sniper and Litening targeting pods as well as JDAM. The test program is currently validating lasing curves for the new pods. The Precision Engagement System (PES) on the A-10C has a digital stores management databus, new cockpit displays and a Situation Awareness Data Link (SADL). The integration of the Joint Direct Attack Munition (JDAM) and Wind Corrected Munitions Dispenser (WCMD) is key to the upgrade along with the introduction of the potent new Sniper pod. Our sister squadron, the 85th TES over at Eglin, has the most heavily instrumented range complex in the US and records data in detail via telemetry that allows analysts back on the ground to monitor data, even down to watching displays in the cockpit. Here we have

overland ranges and a robust threat simulation coupled with the ability to drop live weapons'. Clearly the combination of the two facilities allows the 53rd Wing to ply its testing trade in highly realistic operational environments.

In 2005 the 422nd TES played a key role in a particular Red Flag exercise at Nellis. The squadron regularly supports the 64th AS aggressors during the exercise but for Red Flag 05-4 in August 2005 the 422nd participated specifically to develop tactics and understanding of Net-Centric operations. This is part of the ongoing effort to develop time-sensitive targeting (TST) and Suppression of Enemy Air Defence (SEAD) tactics, enhance CAOC (Combined Air Operations Centre) functionality and decrease sensor-to-shooter time through greater use of datalinks and other communications methods to get decisions from command centres. Lt Col Weed said, 'We managed the south war during Flag. We were looking at ISR (Intelligence, Surveillance and Reconnaissance) strike co-ordination and reconnaissance. We used the new advanced targeting pods in a stand-off role and worked with the CAOC, Joint STARS to develop search patterns for targets for OIF-related requirements'.

Through these operations, the USAF has ensured that it stays at the front line of emerging technology. It also ensures that it maintains its assets and gives the squadrons what they need when they need it.

Above: **End of the day –
a 'Green Bats' F-16CJ returns
to Nellis at the end of the day's
flying.** *Jamie Hunter/AVIACOM*

Right: **A 422nd TES F-16CJ
heads into the break at Nellis
with a Raptor stablemate.**
USAF

Below: **The operational test
squadron 422nd TES paves
the way for the latest
equipment to be introduced to
the front line units. The dark
visor of this F-16 pilot
conceals the concentration of
tanking from a KC-135R.**
Jamie Hunter/AVIACOM

Above: **A 422nd TES F-15C blasts out of Nellis in full reheat for a
test mission. The Eagle carries an AIM-9X on the wing stub pylon
The Suite 5M upgrade for the F-15C has teamed the new missile
with the new helmet-mounted sight in JHMCS.**
Jamie Hunter/AVIACOM

Above: **An immaculate 'Green Bats' F-15C returns to runway 21R at Nellis. The pilot wears the JHMCS helmet.** *Richard Collens*

Left: **This 422nd TES F-15E on the flightline at Nellis carries the new Sniper advanced targeting pod that is replacing the LANTIRN targeting pod on the type. A radar upgrade is also planned for the F-15E and the 'Green Bats' will play a lead role in developing new tactics as well as operationally evaluating the new equipment.** *Jamie Hunter/AVIACOM*

Below left: **Evaluating and integrating the latest weaponry is an important part of the 53rd Wing's work and its associated units. A 422nd TES F-15E climbs out from Nellis toting an array of new weaponry, including the AGM-130 rocket-boosted version of the GBU-15 and a live AGM-154 Joint Stand-Off Weapon (JSOW). The jam-resistant ZSW-1 Improved Datalink Pod (IDLP) on the centreline allows the F-15E crew to control the AGM-130 optically as well as to receive target of opportunity information and imagery in flight under a system known as 'Gold Pan'.** *Jamie Hunter/AVIACOM*

Top: **Framed by Sunrise Mountain, a Maverick-toting 422nd TES A-10A heads out to do battle over the Nellis ranges.** *Jamie Hunter/AVIACOM*

Above: **This 422nd TES F-15E carries an impressive load of six 2,000 lb Mk 84 'iron' bombs during testing.** *Richard Collens*

Right: **Not a regular weapons loadout for the Strike Eagle but typical of the interesting work performed by the 422nd TES, these two F-15Es carry AGM-65 Mavericks.** *Jamie Hunter/AVIACOM*

Left: **Having returned from a test mission, a pair of the 422nd TES' upgraded A-10Cs are met by groundcrews. The squadron was operating three upgraded A-10Cs in September 2005 for flight testing and evaluation of the type's new capabilities.** *Jamie Hunter/AVIACOM*

Right: **The 422nd TES has been testing new Panoramic Night-Vision Goggles (PNVGs) on an A-10 Thunderbolt.** *USAF*

Far right: **The Lockheed Martin Sniper targeting pod is being introduced to the A-10C.** *Jamie Hunter/AVIACOM*

Below: **On the southern live arming area at Nellis, 'OT' A-10C Thunderbolts return from a Close Air Support (CAS) test mission.** *Jamie Hunter/AVIACOM*

Bottom: **One of the 422nd TES' upgraded A-10C test aircraft returns from a mission to evaluate the new Sniper targeting pod on the type.** *Jamie Hunter/AVIACOM*

Chapter Four

NAS Patuxent River

Home of the 'Pax Pioneers'

On the tree-lined banks of the picturesque Chesapeake Bay and its namesake waterway, Naval Air Station Patuxent River in Maryland is the 'spiritual' home of US Naval flight testing and is the headquarters of Naval Air Systems Command (NAVAIR). The station is a hotbed of activity with a diverse array of key US Navy and Marine Corps programs centred here, with testing and evaluation continuing on a daily basis on new aircraft or new system upgrades. Pax River (as it is known) is always a hive of activity, with a number of units based here contributing to the many programs that deliver the latest capabilities to the Navy and Marines.

Commissioned in 1943 in an effort to centralise Naval air testing Patuxent River became the fastest-growing Naval Air Station in the US, now serving as headquarters for the Naval Air Warfare Center Aircraft Division (NAWCAD), and is home to nearly 50 other directorates reporting to the US Navy. Spurred by the events of

World War Two, the farming at Cedar Point, MD, was replaced by flight test operations within a year of the initial plans being drawn up, leading to the Naval Air Test Center being established here on 16 June 1945. The war was instrumental in the evolution of the US Naval test pilot, as combat-experienced aircrews arrived here, leading to formalised classroom instruction starting from 1948 and the establishment of a Test Pilot Training Division. These pilots flew a variety of US-built types, but were also given opportunities to evaluate captured enemy aircraft, including various German and Japanese types, with fleet pilots' tactics being derived from their findings.

From concept to carrier – the US Navy test squadrons at Patuxent River take new aircraft and test them for the front line squadrons to ensure capabilities. *US Navy*

It rapidly became apparent that this facility was going to be pivotal in landmark advances of aviation technology, as the radar tracking, airfield lighting and instrument landing techniques were developed and refined here. Pilots enriched with knowledge gained from the NATC applied their expertise to breakdown the boundaries of flight testing. Of particular note were the first jet aircraft operations at sea, conducted by Lt Cdr James Davidson, flying an FD-1 aboard the USS *Franklin D Roosevelt* in 1946. The innovations of the jet age were evident as over the next few years, speed and altitude records fell as rapidly as they were established. This culminated with Capt W V Davis, then director of the Flight Test Division, becoming the first Navy pilot to exceed the speed of sound on 7 November 1949.

Inset: **The US Navy Test Pilot School patch.**

Centre left: **One of the Test Pilot School F/A-18B Hornets gets airborne from NAS Patuxent River. The Navy TPS provides instruction for new test pilots, flight officers and engineers in the processes and techniques of aircraft and systems test and evaluation. USNTPS operates a diverse fleet of 50 aircraft of 13 different types.**
US Navy/Daniel McLain

Centre right: **TPS instructor Maj Michael Dehner performs a pre-flight walkround check with student Lt Christopher Dotson prior to a systems evaluation mission in the F/A-18B.**
US Navy/Daniel McLain

Left: **A TPS T-2C Buckeye sits ready for take-off as a T-38A undertakes circuit pattern work.** *Jamie Hunter/AVIACOM*

Above: **On the flightline at the Test Pilot School, a T-38A awaits its instructor and student.** *Jamie Hunter/AVIACOM*

Left: **Instructor and student taxi out for a training flight. Interestingly this jet was being flown by a test pilot trainee who is an experienced Top Gun graduate. The TPS publishes manuals for use of the aviation test community for standardisation of flight test techniques and project reporting.** *Jamie Hunter/AVIACOM*

Below: **The secluded TPS flightline at Patuxent River is busy with test operations year-round.** *Jamie Hunter/AVIACOM*

Far left: **Ready for action – one of the School's F/A-18Bs awaits its flight crew. The school's complement of three Hornets is used in the fast jet phase of instruction for both aircrew and engineers.** *Jamie Hunter/AVIACOM*

Left: **The Pratt and Whitney Wasp Junior engine clatters into life as one of the three TPS U-6A Beavers fires up for a mission.** *Jamie Hunter/AVIACOM*

Below left: **A line-up of some the TPS more unusual types, two U-6A Beavers and a U-21F loaned from the US Army for light twin-engined experience for students.** *Jamie Hunter/AVIACOM*

Bottom left: **The old Navy training workhorse the T-2C Buckeye is still maintained by the TPS due to its excellent handling and flexibility.** *Jamie Hunter/AVIACOM*

Right: **The basic layout of the front cockpit of the venerable T-2C Buckeye.** *Jamie Hunter/AVIACOM*

Below: **A number of Bell OH-50C Kiowas are on loan from the US Army for rotary test pilot training with the School.** *Jamie Hunter/AVIACOM*

Right: **The TPS operates the US Navy's only T-38s, acquired from the USAF. These have now been upgraded to T-38C standard with new avionics.** *Jamie Hunter/AVIACOM*

Bottom: **One of the Test Pilot School's immaculate F/A-18B Hornets.** *Jamie Hunter/AVIACOM*

As is usually the case, a conflict motivates rapid advances in military technology and the Korean War period enabled the Navy to flex its modern jet muscle at sea, guided missiles replaced cannons and military aviation was taking quantum leaps forward.

The US Navy Test Pilot School was established here in 1958 and its potential was quickly realised when four of the seven astronauts selected to join the space race in 1959 were graduates of the school. Indeed, in 1961 former Navy test pilot and TPS graduate Alan Shepard became the first American in space.

A sweeping reorganisation and restructuring process came into effect here in 1975, preparing the NATC for its role as the principal site for development testing under the control of NAVAIR and by 1991 it was all change again. Further consolidation designed to improve products and services resulted in the formation of the Naval Air Warfare Center (NAWC). The main element of the Aircraft Division at Patuxent River branches out into four efficient sub-divisions; VX-23 Strike Aircraft Test, VX-20 Force Aircraft, HX-21 Rotary Wing Test and the Test Pilots School, each supported by the Test and Evaluation Group (TEAM) born from the original Systems Test directorate. Today these units are collectively known as Test Wing Atlantic and they serve to effectively bridge the gap between the manufacturer and the carrier deck.

TPS – PUSHING THE BOUNDARIES

The US Naval Test Pilot School typically runs two courses in parallel over an 11 month period, training Navy, Marine, Air Force and Army officers as well as foreign nationals and civil service engineers how to test. The unit maintains a variety of aircraft and airborne systems capabilities necessary to train efficient test pilots and engineers. The School not only provides fixed-wing aircrew, but also helicopter test pilots which is the only source for the US Government or Industry. As well as the training of new pilots and engineers in the testing environment, the School investigates and develops new flight testing techniques. Fixed Wing, Rotary Wing and Systems students all work together to promote greater understanding for future 'live' testing. Fixed Wing students can expect to enter into

initial handling evaluations on the T-2 Buckeye and T-38 Talon to promote greater awareness of aircraft handling in order to effectively glean flight test data. The OH-6 Cayuse and the OH-58 Kiowa provide similar tasks for the Rotary Wing students. The Systems students are exposed to cutting-edge technology which includes the ability to evaluate live data in a classroom-type environment aboard the school's NP-3D 'El Coyote' which is equipped with an F-16 APG-68 radar, representing advanced technology that students would expect to encounter in the operational trials field. The aircraft is also fitted with a dummy cockpit to prepare Systems students for future live-fly missions teamed up with their Fixed Wing colleagues working together in the School's F/A-18 Hornets.

The first of six T-6A Texan IIs for the TPS arrived at Patuxent River in September 2005, to start replacing the venerable T-2 Buckeyes. TPS commander Lt Col Steve Kihara commented, 'Each type of aircraft assigned to TPS brings a unique set of performance, handling, or systems qualities that are used to satisfy a particular set of learning objectives in the syllabus. The T-6 is one of the two primary aircraft for the fixed-wing curriculum replacing long-time TPS favourite, the T-2 Buckeye. Beginning with Class 131, students will fly the Texan II along with the T-38. Test Pilot School has been looking for a few years to replace its soon-to-be obsolete T-2 inventory. The Buckeye has been an incredible tool for teaching Naval aviators to be test pilots, especially the dynamics of inverted spins. But since the Navy T-2 fleet is quickly declining, it has become more expensive to maintain and operate making it improbable that TPS could financially keep the T-2s as useful tools. Having fixed-wing students learn the characteristics of both turboprop aircraft and jet flying, the T-6 and T-38 combination will help TPS produce test pilots who

have more experience. The Texan's digital cockpit will provide a training advantage over the T-2's analogue instrumentation. Today's test pilots need to be trained to test tomorrow's aircraft. The T-6 instantly provides a modern systems platform with ready capabilities for our system students'.

SALTY DOGS

Like its sister Naval flight test and evaluation squadrons, the Strike Aircraft Test Squadron 'Salty Dogs' was given a numeric identity on 1 May 2002. Today known as VX-23, it is NAWC's largest flight test organisation, conducting research, development, test and evaluation of fixed wing tactical aircraft in the Navy and Marines inventory. The squadron flies a mixed fleet comprising F/A-18A to D Hornets, F/A-18E/F Super Hornets, an EA-6B Prowler and a T-45C Goshawk, conducting over 3,000 flight operations annually, totalling about 5,000 flight hours of high-risk flight test. The squadron is heavily involved in the continued development of the Boeing F/A-18E/F Super Hornet as well as upgrades to the 'Legacy' F/A-18 Hornet and also recently the Northrop Grumman EA-6B Prowler ICAP-III upgrade. ICAP-III (Increased Capability III) is designed to increase the type's ability to defeat next-generation missile and electronic threats through the enhanced ALQ-99 tactical jamming system and it reached Initial Operating Capability (IOC) in 2005 following its operational evaluation (OPEVAL).

Patuxent River is the principal site for the development testing of the Super Hornet. Since the first flight of the type on 29 September 1995, the rigorous flight test program at Pax escalated to utilise seven test airframes; five single-seat E models and two twin-seat

Above: **Boeing F/A-18E Super Hornets at VX-23 between trials missions.** *Jamie Hunter/AVIACOM*

Left: **An F/A-18C Hornet of VX-23 'Salty Dogs' releases Mk 83 1,000 lb bombs during a series of tests for the Advanced Targeting Forward Looking Infra-Red (ATFLIR) over the Atlantic Test Range. Tests are designed to evaluate the safe separation of various weapons when released adjacent to the ATFLIR system on the F/A-18C/D.** *US Navy/Vernon Pugh*

The heavily-instrumented second F/A-18E (E2) loaded with Mk 82 bombs returns from a test mission over the Atlantic test ranges.
Ted Carlson/Fotodynamics

F models. Each aircraft was individually fitted out for specific tasking with instrumentation specifically designed for each test requirement. The mid-Atlantic Test and Training Range adjacent to Pax River offers datalink systems feeding back real-time information so that such testing can enjoy the benefits of ground-based systems analysts fully evaluating each mission on a live basis. Such test missions can be extremely complex, sometimes up to 70 tasks can be completed on a flight that could last up to five hours. Early Super Hornet testing revealed a wholly satisfactory product, with the only negative flight characteristic being a wing drop tendency at high angles of attack, which was subsequently rectified thanks to wing leading edge modifications. Taking the Super Hornet to sea was also a task set for the integrated contractor/Navy test team at Pax River. Initial land-based catapult launches and arrestings as well as steam ingestion tests and jet blast deflector trials were followed by the first F/A-18F (F1) embarking the USS *John C Stennis* on 17 January 1997 for the first all-important carrier suitability trials.

Weapons separation trials are also a key task falling to VX-23. For the Super Hornet in particular this involved the delivery of over 50 different types of ordnance. With its greater range, endurance and enhanced survivability over the 'Legacy' Hornet the type has proved extremely successful as it replaces the F-14 Tomcat in fleet service. Sadly in 2005 the F-14 is no longer on strength at VX-23, with Tomcat testing having all but halted as the type nears final retirement in

2006. However in May 2005 VX-23 welcomed back two F-14Ds from VF-101 'Grim Reapers' for one last trial. With VX-30 'Bloodhounds' at NBVC Point Mugu having retired its last test F-14s, the 'Grim Reapers' bought the F-14 back to Pax River to introduce the 500 lb GBU-38 JDAM to the F-14D's arsenal ready for the last-ever operational deployment for the type. The commander of VF-213 'Black Lions' expressed an interest in his unit carrying and employing the smallest JDAM variant, in addition to the 2,000 lb GBU-31 it already used. NAVAIR swung into action and VF-101 stepped in to fill the unanticipated requirement for F-14D test aircraft, led by commanding officer Cdr Paul Haas. Testing began on 11 May following a short requalification by VF-101 for F-14 experienced VX-23 test aircrew. Led by Test Wing Atlantic Ordnance Support Team boss Cdr Eric 'Pinto' Mitchell and VX-23 test RIO (Radar Intercept Officer) Lt Kevin 'Lamb' Watkins, captive carriage was completed during the first day of flight testing and separation was completed the following day, dropping a pair of GBU-38s on the inshore-instrumented range. Carrier suitability testing, consisting of high-rate-of-descent arrested landings, was completed in just one day and VX-23 paved the way for completion of two guided weapon releases at China Lake in June.

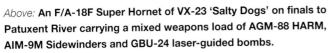

Above: **An F/A-18F Super Hornet of VX-23 'Salty Dogs' on finals to Patuxent River carrying a mixed weapons load of AGM-88 HARM, AIM-9M Sidewinders and GBU-24 laser-guided bombs.** *US Navy/Joe Hegedus*

Above right: **Carrying a full load of four AGM-154 Joint Stand-Off Missiles (JSOW), this F/A-18C conducts early trials for the missile. JSOW is a GPS-guided glide bomb with wings that pop out and was first used operationally in Operation *Southern Watch* over Iraq in 1999.** *US Navy*

Right: **Detached to the sister station at NAWS China Lake in the Mojave Desert, this F/A-18C of VX-23 conducts AIM-9X test firing. As seen here, weapons release trials usually mean that the trials aircraft is fitted with a variety of high-speed cameras for recording release phases for post-flight analysis.** *US Navy/Raytheon*

Below: **Ground flight test engineers prepare a VX-23 F/A-18E for a test mission.** *Jamie Hunter/AVIACOM*

Left: **Fitted with multiple ejector racks, a VX-23 F/A-18B heads out, piloted by one of the Marine Corps test pilots on Strike's aircrew team.** *Jamie Hunter/AVIACOM*

Below left: **'Salty Dog 112', an F/A-18A from VX-23, takes time out to pose for the camera during a trials sortie from Pax.** *Jamie Hunter/AVIACOM*

Bottom: **A deck marshaller guides an F/A-18F Super Hornet of VX-23 onto the catapult for launch during flightdeck operations trials aboard USS *Theodore Roosevelt* (CVN-71).** *US Navy/Eben Boothby*

Right: **A VX-23 F/A-18A Hornet makes the first-ever 'trap' aboard the nuclear-powered aircraft carrier USS *Ronald Reagan* (CVN-76) as the squadron undertakes part of the ship's initial flightdeck certification process.** *US Navy/Frankie Bridges*

Far right: **This 'Salty Dogs' EA-6B Prowler has been heavily involved in the ICAP-III upgrade that will give the type new capabilities in order for it to stay potent until around 2015 when it is replaced by the EA-18G.** *Jamie Hunter/AVIACOM*

Right: **VX-23 operates this smart T-45C Goshawk for trials of the advanced trainer.** *Ted Carlson/Fotodynamics*

Below right: **VX-23 Strike Test Squadron's Digital Flight Control System (DFCS) F-14A Tomcat has long been retired, however, the US Navy bought a pair of F-14Ds back to Patuxent River in 2005 for one last series of trials to clear the GBU-38 for carriage by the type. This example is seen formating on a VX-20 KC-130F during AIM-54 Phoenix release trials in the outer Atlantic Test Range during happier times.** *Jamie Hunter/AVIACOM*

PAX X-Planes

Below: **The experimental X-31 returns to Pax River following a test flight for the VECTOR (Vectoring Extremely Short Take-off and Landing Control Tailless Operation Research) program. The X-31 used thrust vectoring to maintain control at high angles of attack and reduced speeds in the landing configuration.** *USMC/Maj Cody Allee*

Below: **The Boeing X-32B was the STOVL version of the concept demonstrator beaten for the Joint Strike Fighter (JSF) competition by the X-35. The X-32B now sits in the museum at Patuxent River.** *US Navy*

Right: **The future at Patuxent River. The Lockheed Martin X-35C concept demonstrator for the carrier version (CV) of the JSF cruises above Patuxent River in 2001 piloted by Maj Art Tomassetti during carrier suitability trials. The F-35 will return here for extensive testing during the next phase of testing from 2007 as the concept turns into the next US Navy fleet fighter to replace the 'Legacy' Hornet.** *Lockheed Martin*

FORCE FLYERS

The Force Aircraft Test Squadron VX-20 operates in much the same way as VX-23, but concentrates on the larger end of the aircraft spectrum with a fleet of P-3 Orions, C-130 Hercules and E-2 Hawkeyes. All major projects are instigated with a tasking statement from NAVAIR and reports are drawn up from project managers, aircrew and engineers with collated research data. Like all test squadrons, VX-20 is at the forefront of new technology for its assigned aircraft. The next-generation E-2D Advanced Hawkeye airborne early warning aircraft is now in the System Development and Demonstration (SDD) phase here. This $1.9bn contract is for two new-build Advanced Hawkeyes, which are slated to enter operational testing by 2007 with a new UHF Electronically Steerable Array (UESA) radar, tactical cockpit, new communications suite and a surveillance infra-red search and track system to detect theatre ballistic missiles. The US Navy eventually plans to procure up to 75 new-build examples, with full operating capability planned for 2015-2017.

Left: **A VX-20 Force Aircraft Test Squadron P-3C Orion AIP (Anti-surface warfare Improvement Program) still bearing old NAWC markings on the fin, fires up for a local pilot proficiency 'hop'.** *Jamie Hunter/AVIACOM*

Above: **The eight-bladed Hamilton Sundstrand NP2000 propellers are particularly evident on the VX-20 test E-2C Hawkeye 2000, seen here during Field Carrier Landing Practice (FCLP). The NP2000 program is introducing the new propellers for the E-2C as well as the C-2A Greyhound.** *Jamie Hunter/AVIACOM*

Top right: **High above NAS Patuxent River, a VX-20 E-2C heads out for a test mission on a crystal-clear afternoon.** *US Navy*

Centre right: **VX-20's NC-130H Hercules provides an in-flight testbed for the E-2 Hawkeye Radar Modernization Program (RMP) currently under development. Lockheed Martin will produce five radar systems that will be used for qualification, reliability and flight testing, followed by a full-scale production program that will outfit 75 aircraft in the E-2C fleet by 2020.** *US Navy*

Right: **A C-2A Greyhound is kept on strength at VX-20 for ongoing tests, with new NP2000 propellers now being added.** *US Navy*

The US Marine Corps' KC-130J next-generation aerial refuelling tanker aircraft has recently successfully passed a second phase of operational evaluation following initial development work at VX-20. The squadron has been central to developing the new capabilities of the type with improved reliability and maintainability, increased mission availability and improved delivery of fuel, with the US Navy commander of Operational Testing and Evaluation (OT&E) having recommended 'full fleet introduction'.

Above: **S-3B Vikings of VX-20 and VX-1 fly near Patuxent River. These aircraft were the last remaining Patuxent River-based S-3Bs in 2004 and were transferred to the fleet on completion of the last testing for the type.** *US Navy*

Left: **A Force (VX-20) KC-130F returns to Patuxent River following a mission providing aerial tanker support for testing.** *Ted Carlson/Fotodynamics*

Below left: **Despite being operated in fast-dwindling numbers by the US Navy the P-3C Orion is still receiving upgrades that are in test with VX-20. The overland surveillance role as well as the anti-surface warfare improvement program (AIP) have been significant projects in recent years. The type is slated to be replaced in service by the Boeing P-8A Multi-mission Maritime Aircraft (MMA).** *Jamie Hunter/AVIACOM*

Top right: **This early NP-3D is attached to the Naval Research Laboratory (NRL) Flight Support Detachment at Patuxent River. The NRL operates five uniquely modified P-3 Orions as airborne research platforms. Formed in July 1965 as the Oceanographic Air Survey Unit (OASU) this unit is dedicated to airborne geophysical survey work. In December 2004, the unit at Patuxent River became Scientific Development Squadron One (VXS-1).** *Jamie Hunter/AVIACOM*

Right: **The MH-60R Seahawk, the US Navy's next-generation submarine hunter and surface attack helicopter to replace the SH-60B/F Seahawk, entered operational evaluation at Patuxent River with VX-1 in May 2005.** *Ted Carlson/Fotodynamics*

HX-21 'BLACKJACK'

The Naval Rotary Wing Aircraft Test Squadron HX-21 'Blackjack' is located next door to the Test Pilot School and it provides a vital service for the extensive US Naval and Marine Corps rotary fleet. The unit is primarily responsible for development testing and evaluation of all new rotary projects for these two services and also provides support for US Army and USAF rotary testing at its unique facilities to avoid duplicating trials for similar type aircraft. It makes for a busy and diverse schedule here, especially considering the sheer number of new helicopter projects that are currently running.

An integrated V-22 Osprey test team comprised of Bell, Boeing, and US military personnel was formed at Patuxent River in November 1993 for the development of this radical new type aircraft under the jurisdiction of HX-21. Under the command of Lt Col Keith Danel in 2005, HX-21 is now directly involved in MV-22B testing and the squadron is extremely busy with this and the Navy's many other new programs. In 2004 the squadron conducted almost twice the average number of flight and ground test hours as in the previous 20 years. The squadron operates six MV-22B, a single CH-53E Super Stallion has recently been used to test a new ramp-mounted 0.50 calibre door gun, TH-57C Jet Rangers are used for chase and continuation training and a unique Sikorsky NVH-3A with some software common with the Presidential VH-60 allows certain validations to be performed. The squadron's most numerous types are

a host of Sikorsky H-60 Seahawk family variants. The US Navy's huge fleet standardisation effort that is well under way will ultimately lead to just two helicopter types in service – the Sikorsky MH-60R Seahawk and the MH-60S KnightHawk.

The MH-60R program calls for 243 mostly new-build examples, with the type combining the capabilities of the SH-60B and the SH-60F as well as sporting a host of new technology, including the Lockheed Martin common glass cockpit that it shares with the MH-60S. MH-60R is the Navy's next-generation submarine hunter and surface attack helicopter, having entered operational evaluation on 9 May 2005 with VX-1 'Pioneers' at Pax River following extensive testing at HX-21. Designed to directly replace the

Left: **HX-21 'Blackjack' operates six MV-22B Ospreys for continued development testing of the type for the US Marines.** *Ted Carlson/Fotodynamics*

Right: **A US Marine Corps MV-22B Osprey of the NAVAIR V-22 Integrated Test Team (ITT) departs Patuxent River for a test mission. The MV-22 advanced Vertical/Short Take-Off and Landing (VSTOL) multipurpose aircraft is replacing the CH-46E Sea Knight and CH-53D Sea Stallion in service.** *US Navy/Daniel McLain*

Left: **On the flightline at HX-21 'Blackjack', a test MH-60R and USMC CH-53E Super Stallion.** *Jamie Hunter/AVIACOM*

Below: **An MV-22 from Marine Tilt-rotor Test and Evaluation Squadron HMX-22 operating near Nellis AFB to assess performance in austere environments. Following two fatal crashes in 2000 of LRIP MV-22Bs the test Osprey fleet was grounded pending safety improvement studies. The program is now back on track towards full operational capability.** *US Navy*

SH-60B and SH-60F, Lockheed Martin is the mission systems integrator for the MH-60R and its new mission systems underwent a six-month developmental test (DT) phase, known as technical evaluation, with HX-21.

In 2002, full rate production for 237 new MH-60S was granted and the type is now in service with the Navy and is now fulfilling its (Block 1) vertical replenishment (VERTREP) fleet role replacing the venerable CH-46 Sea Knight. The rotary test team at HX-21 is now concentrating on development of two new missions for this versatile helicopter. The need for a more rapidly deployable mine warfare platform and the desire to operate just two types, meant that the capability has turned to the MH-60S. The MH-60S Block 2A/B will eventually replace the MH-53E Sea Dragon and take on the mission to detect and destroy mines to clear the path for the battle groups under the Organic Airborne Mine Countermeasures (OAMCM) program. Five subsystems comprise OAMCM. Northrop Grumman's Airborne Laser Mine Detection System (ALMDS) uses a light detecting and ranging laser to detect, localise and classify near-surface, moored and floating sea mines. The AN/AQS-20A towed sonar is designed to be deployed from the hover and towed by a MH-60S to detect, localise, and classify mines and is a development of the AN/AQS-14 towed sensor package. The Organic Airborne Surface Influence Sweep (OASIS) system is designed to deploy from a hovering helicopter and to be towed at high speeds in shallow water in support of limited mine clearance operations. The Airborne Mine Neutralisation System (AMNS) is a non-towed mine system designed to destroy unburied bottom and moored sea mines. Originally developed for use on the MH-53E, this neutralisation system uses sonar and video sensors enclosed in a torpedo-shaped body allowing the

aircraft sensor operator to guide the sensor to the body and identify the target prior to operator-commanded detonation of the torpedo warhead and mine. Finally, the Rapid Airborne Mine Clearance System fires a supercavitating projectile from a Bushmaster II Mk 44 gun aboard the MH-60S. The towpoint installation is an extensive structural modification to the baseline of the MH-60S airframe. This modification will allow the airframe to safely and efficiently absorb expected loads during the tow missions. Contractor integration testing, including ground and flight integration of the five individual mission subsystems is undertaken by the Naval Surface Warfare Center Coastal Systems Station (CSS), Panama City, FL, and by HX-21.

A further role for the MH-60S comes under Block 3 – which includes special operations (SPECWAR) and 'armed helicopter' roles. The latter of these is currently in the planning phase and could be on the fleet by 2007. This will see the MH-60S having an expanded capability over the current HH-60H and will see the type fitted with FLIR, guns and Hellfire missiles. MH-60S Armed Helicopter Weapons System (AHWS) was unveiled in late 2004 and will provide future expeditionary strike group commanders with robust capability in the areas of organic combat search and rescue, maritime interdiction operations, surface warfare and aircraft carrier 'plane guard' SAR duties. Weapon capabilities include eight Hellfire missiles carried on external weapon system wings and the AN/AAS-44C forward-looking infra-red system. Additionally, the mission kit will give the crew capability to fire FN-Herstal's laser-sighted 7.62mm guns from the port and starboard cabin windows and laser-sighted GAU-21, 0.50 calibre guns from the port and starboard cabin doors. Sikorsky has installed the first two AHWS mission kits and the system will complete a rigorous test program until summer of 2006 ahead of initial operational capability.

The future for 'Blackjack' looks set to be positive with huge new programs coming along. The squadron will be heavily involved with AgustaWestland/Lockheed Martin VH-71A Future Presidential helicopter to replace the VH-3 and VH-60 from 2009. Flight testing is scheduled to begin at Patuxent River in 2006. In addition, the US Marine Corps' CH-53E replacement will involve extensive testing at HX-21 for the planned new Sikorsky CH-53F.

NEW HUEYS

The US Marine Corps' helicopter inventory, like that of the Navy, is being upgraded on an unprecedented scale. At Patuxent River the Bell Textron H-1 Upgrade program has a 140-strong Bell-Government Integrated Test Team for the Engineering Manufacturing Development (EMD) phase devoted to the new UH-1Y and AH-1Z Cobra helicopter modernisation programs. This effort was initially planned to entail the remanufacture of 280 UH-1Ns and AH-1Ws to the vastly improved new configurations. However, operational tempo and cost considerations have now moved this to a new-build program.

The H-1 upgrade is designed to address power and fatigue issues as well as introduce new capabilities – it also gives the two types an incredible 84% commonality. The two UH-1Ys and three AH-1Zs at Patuxent River have conducted everything from handling to weapons implementation trials. The first shipboard test operations were conducted aboard amphibious assault ship USS *Bataan* (LHD-5) off the Virginia Capes with 267 landings completed during

Left: **The MH-60S Armed Helicopter Weapons System (AHWS) was unveiled in late 2004 and weapons capabilities include eight Hellfire missiles as illustrated here.** *US Navy*

Bottom left: **Bell AH-1Z 'Zulu One' returns from a handling test flight at Pax River. The US Marine Corps AH-1Z includes the Thales TopOwl Helmet-Mounted Sighting System (HMSS) and glass cockpit.** *Jamie Hunter/AVIACOM*

Right: **A UH-1Y comes in to land during the first shipboard test operations aboard amphibious assault ship USS *Bataan* (LHD-5).** *US Navy*

Below: **The AH-1Z and UH-1Y on the deck lift of USS *Bataan* (LHD-5) during sea trials. Note the re-designed horizontal engine exhausts on both models.** *US Navy*

nearly 30 flight hours in both day and night operations. The two types were being tested for their capacity to 'live aboard' the ship. A design reconfiguration phase for the two types came as the result of flight testing, with a number of refinements introduced. The upgraded H-1 includes the Thales TopOwl Helmet-Mounted Sighting System (HMSS) and glass cockpit. The TopOwl system will be slaved to the gun and the AGM-114 Hellfire missiles on the AH-1Z as well as 2.75in rockets and waist-mounted guns on the UH-1Y. The new General Electric T700 engines and composite rotor head give incredible new performance, with twice the range or payload now possible.

In October 2005 the Marine Corps and NAVAIR accepted the first AH-1Z and UH-1Y for Operational Evaluation (OPEVAL) at Pax River to begin in early 2006.

Left: **An HX-21 'Blackjack' MH-60R deploys its dipping sonar during trials at the Atlantic Undersea Test and Evaluation Center (AUTEC) Bahamas in February 2005 to complete its final acoustics test period for technical evaluation.** *US Navy*

Above: **This MH-60R (BuNo 166404) is the third Low Rate Initial Production (LRIP) new build example from Sikorsky and is used for flight testing with HX-21 at Patuxent River.** *Jamie Hunter/AVIACOM*

Below: **Lt Jeff Farlin of HX-21 hits the emergency jettison button to release as AN/AQS-20 test vehicle from its carriage position during daytime flight test over the Atlantic Test Range Chesapeake Bay Restricted Areas.** *US Navy*

Left: **An MH-60S comes in to land at an austere site during flight testing with HX-21. The type will be used for US Navy special operations warfare (SPECWAR).** *US Navy*

Above: **The US Navy is rationalising helicopter fleets under the common Sikorsky MH-60, to be implemented over a twelve-year period this will combine three helicopter communities into two and increase the number of fleet squadrons by six to 31. HSM squadrons will operate four MH-60Rs from aircraft carriers and eight from the escorting cruisers and destroyers. HSC squadrons will operate six MH-60Ss from the carrier and two from the logistics ship that service the strike group. Five other HSM squadrons will fill an expeditionary role, deploying their MH-60Rs in small detachments on board cruisers, destroyers, and littoral combat ships in expeditionary strike groups or steaming independently. The MH-60S is also set to replace the MH-53E Sea Dragon mine countermeasures helicopters used by two Helicopter Mine Countermeasures (HM) squadrons, however the exact plans for this are undecided.** *Ted Carlson/Fotodynamics*

Top left: **Patuxent River's Search and Rescue (SAR) Flight operates this UH-3H Sea King. It is also used to evaluate new water rescue techniques.** *US Navy/James Darcy*

Centre left: **HX-21 also has the use of TH-57Cs for camera chase duties and for continuation training.** *Ted Carlson/Fotodynamics*

Left: **The US Marine Corps is to receive 23 AgustaWestland/ Lockheed Martin VH-71A (US101) helicopters for the Presidential transport role. The type will be extensively tested by HX-21.** *Team US101*

UAVS AT PAX

Reflecting the inevitable unmanned future of certain aspects of military aviation, Patuxent River is hosting no less than eight UAV types involved in evaluative programs. Among these, the Northrop Grumman RQ-8A Fire Scout VTUAV (Vertical Take-Off and Landing UAV) is being tested for shipborne operations, and following its maiden flight in 2004, the Global Hawk Maritime Demonstration aircraft, part of NAVAIR's Unmanned Aerial Vehicles program (PMA-263) is now due here. Capt Paul Morgan commented, 'This is a system not just an air vehicle. This maritime demonstration program is meant to support the fleet in exercises of their choosing in order to work through the tactics and the procedures of how we're going to operate the Broad Area Maritime Surveillance (BAMS) unmanned air systems, which is the follow-on'. The RQ-4 demonstration here is scheduled to last for several years, incorporating fleet exercises as the Navy evaluates its requirement for a high-altitude, long-endurance unmanned aerial system capability as an asset to provide persistent intelligence, surveillance and reconnaissance. Global Hawk gives the fleet over-the-horizon reconnaissance capability and its sensor array can feed back vital information. Whereas the Pioneer or Fire Scout UAVs can relay usable data real-time, the Global Hawk is more like being fed by Niagra Falls, there's a huge amount of data.

Above: **A Marine Security Force (MSF) soldier practises Fast Rope exercises from an MH-60S Knighthawk of VX-1 at Patuxent River.** *US Navy*

Below: **A VX-1 'Pioneers' MH-60R fires a Hellfire missile during operational testing.** *US Navy/VX-1*

Chapter Five

China Lake

Dust Devils and Vampires of the Desert

The arid Mojave desert in California isn't necessarily the first location that springs to mind as a place to find the US Navy at work. However, this very area has long been associated with military flight testing, with its year-round good weather and desolate landscape providing an ideal environment for such activities. This rugged desert area features famous installations such as the Lockheed Martin Skunk Works at Plant 42 in Palmdale and of course Edwards AFB. The US Navy is here as well, tucked away adjacent to the high desert town of Ridgecrest – nestling on the desert floor in sight of the imposing Sierra Nevada mountains is NAWS China Lake. This important naval station is home to Naval Air Warfare Center (NAWC) Weapons Division, a vast sprawling complex of scientific laboratories and test installations as well as Armitage Field – the home of the two important flight test squadrons here. On a daily basis VX-31 'Dust Devils' and VX-9 'Vampires' launch waves of missions to put the latest systems and weapons to the test on the vast China Lake complex of electronic and impact ranges. China Lake's ranges challenge new systems and are punished daily by advanced munitions dedicated to ensuring that the US Navy and Marine Corps stay at the cutting edge. Along with its sister weapons station at Point Mugu, China Lake clearly plays a unique and important role for the modern US Navy.

'The Lake', as it is fondly known to the personnel here, is undoubtedly one of the most impressive military installations in existence. Its location is impressive, its secrecy is impressive and its importance is impressive – it's just got an impressive aura about it. China Lake is a precious asset for the US Navy. It is a complete test and evaluation facility for NAVAIR with more than one million acres of desert and uncluttered airspace. The few hotels are packed out with contractors or visiting military personnel and 'Charlie's' sports bar has become something of a shrine, decked out with photos and memorabilia from visiting squadrons.

The US Navy first came here during World War Two in 1943 when the Naval Ordnance Test Station (NOTS) was first established to test

rockets under development by the California Institute of Technology (Caltech), the US Navy also needed a new proving ground for all aviation ordnance. Testing began at China Lake within a month of being established, with the sparsely-populated desert around China Lake and Inyokern proving absolutely ideal for the secret development and evaluation of new weapons. With a mixture of both military and civilian collaboration, the work at NOTS rapidly expanded to include research, development, test and evaluation of missiles, torpedoes, guns, bombs, and fuses and even NASA's Lunar Soft Landing Vehicle.

In July 1967 NOTS China Lake and the Naval Ordnance Laboratory, CA, became the Naval Weapons Center (NWC), with activities consolidated at 'The Lake' in 1971. Over the following years, the US Navy strike attack fleet plied its trade here pushing capabilities ever further, with A-4 Skyhawks, A-6 Intruders and A-7 Corsairs amongst the most prolific types in the skies over and around the base. In January 1992, the Naval Weapons Center at China Lake and the Pacific Missile Test Center (PMTC) at Point Mugu were disestablished and combined as a single command, the Naval Air Warfare Center Weapons Division (NAWCWPNS) of today. NAWC has had to be versatile and able to fulfil a multitude of diverse and challenging programs assigned by the overseeing NAVAIR directorate.

The Weapons Division of today boasts an impressive track record of weapons development, having played leading roles in the development of cluster weapons, Tomahawk cruise missiles, laser-guided 'smart' bombs, the Global Positioning System (GPS) guided Joint Direct Attack Munition (JDAM), as well as many well-known munitions such as Shrike, HARM, Phoenix, Walleye, Maverick and Sparrow. The famous Sidewinder air-to-air heat-seeking missile was also developed here, with subsequent generations of this hugely successful weapon all having been carried and fired from China Lake trials aircraft. The divisions here and at Point Mugu can carry out the complete weapon development process, from basic and applied research through to prototypes and onto the operational arena. It's not just weapons that are tested here, with electronic warfare, threat detection and countermeasures, night attack

Devil's work – led by Cdr Bill Chubb, CO of VX-31 until September 2005, in his F/A-18F with Cdr Tim Morey, his successor, following in an F/A-18E on a mission from China Lake.
Jamie Hunter/AVIACOM

Above: **Flown by Lt Cdr 'Doc' Shoemaker with Cdr Bill Chubb in the back seat, VX-31 Boeing F/A-18F Super Hornet (radio callsign 'Coso 51') is seen over the snow-capped Sierra Nevada near China Lake.** *Jamie Hunter/AVIACOM*

Right: **Over 'The Lake'. A section of VX-31 'Dust Devils' fighters sweep low over the famous base.** *Jamie Hunter/AVIACOM*

systems, ejector seats and parachutes illustrating the diverse portfolio boasted by these Naval testers.

On 8 May 1995, the main development flight test squadron at China Lake became known as Naval Weapons Test Squadron China Lake 'Dust Devils' thanks to a command re-shuffle, followed in May 2002 with the addition of the Air Test and Evaluation Squadron (AIRTEVRON) designation, with the China Lake unit becoming VX-31 (AIRTEVRON Three One) 'Dust Devils'. This elite unit has a long history of test and evaluation with the Weapons Division, working in tandem with manufacturers and contractors in support of the US Naval fleet. The test units at China Lake have major bearing on programs such as electronic warfare, threat detection, countermeasures, night attack systems, ejector seats and parachutes. The Weapons Division here carries out the complete weapon development process, from basic and applied research through to prototypes and onto the operational arena.

Left: **Looking out across the VX-31 and VX-9 flightline at China Lake, with the imposing Sierra Nevada mountains in the distance.** *Jamie Hunter/AVIACOM*

Below left: **A 'Dust Devils' test pilot climbs aboard his 'Rhino' for a test mission.** *Jamie Hunter/AVIACOM*

Below: **In the hot seat – the author in the back seat of 'Dust Devil' F/A-18F '214' callsign 'Coso 52' lined up and ready to depart from runway 21 at China Lake. The acceleration in the Super Hornet is brisk to say the least, with a real kick in the back for a full 'burner' take-off.** *Jamie Hunter/AVIACOM*

DEVIL'S WORK

The 'Dust Devils' of VX-31 maintain a stable of approximately 25 highly instrumented aircraft to support its mission, including around 15 Boeing F/A-18A to D Hornets and F/A-18E/F Super Hornets, five Boeing AV-8B Harrier IIs, a Bell AH-1W Cobra, a T-39 Sabreliner, two Fairchild Metroliners and three Bell HH-1N search and rescue helicopters. The squadron's pilots log approximately 4,200 hours of test and training flights each year, most of which are in support of aircraft weapons integration programs.

In 2004 the squadron was commanded by Cdr Bill Chubb, with his squadron being fuelled by Air Tasking Orders generated by NAVAIR to provide the squadron with anything from a brief overview of a problem that requires attention, to a precise element of a program that they will manage, working with a manufacturer or as a separate entity. The nature of the work undertaken by the squadron means that some aircrew are graduate Test Pilots and others experienced fleet aviators, this allows a broad opinion over the effectiveness of a project. The mission of VX-31 differs from the Aircraft Division's VX-23 at Patuxent River, which has a primary

Left: **Heading out for a test mission toting AIM-7 Sparrow missiles, a VX-31 F-model 'Rhino' blasts out from China Lake in full afterburner.** *Jamie Hunter/AVIACOM*

mission of testing and refining aircraft systems, flying qualities, performance, safe weapon separation and carrier suitability. As Cdr Chubb explained, 'As the Developmental Test Squadron that makes up Naval Air Warfare Center Weapons Division, VX-31's primary mission is integrating software and weapon systems onto our various weapons platforms. We have a huge diversity of ongoing programs and weapon systems that are being developed at VX-31 such as AARGM (AGM-88E Advanced Anti-Radiation Guided Missile), AGM-154 JSOW-C (Joint Stand-Off Weapon), JDAM (Joint Direct Attack Munition) with anti-GPS jamming enhancements and the Raytheon AIM-9X'. The AGM-88E AARGM is a particularly significant program for the US Navy and is a follow-on to the AGM-88 High-Speed Anti-Radiation Missile (HARM). AARGM has a new dual-mode seeker that will be able to target radar sites even if they shut down, a huge leap in capability over HARM and critical to reducing collateral damage. The Navy has started captive-carry flight tests of the prototype of the millimetre-wave radar for the multimode seeker of the AGM-88E AARGM and the test program, which started in October 2004, led to a preliminary design review in March 2005, to be followed by a critical design review in March 2006. The massive $228m AARGM effort will enter operational evaluation in 2008 and initial operational capability in 2009 loaded aboard the potent F/A-18C/D and F/A-18E/F Hornet family.

RAMPANT RHINO

Much of VX-31's test work in 2005 is geared towards the Navy's biggest and newest strike fighter aircraft – the Boeing F/A-18E/F Super Hornet. The Super Hornet, or 'Rhino' as it is becoming affectionately known, represents a cost-effective solution to Navy requirements for a versatile and adaptable performer, born out of a need to improve load and range capabilities over the 'Legacy' Hornet. The Super Hornet is fast replacing the Grumman F-14 Tomcat in service, as well as superseding some 'Legacy' Hornets in a number of fleet squadrons. The Super Hornet is already showing its worth, it has struck targets in combat with precision, it is replacing the S-3B Viking as a tanker and it is also set to replace the EA-6B Prowler in the Navy fleet in the future. The Super Hornet has huge growth potential, and is consequently receiving a wealth of new technology as it matures.

The 'Dust Devils' have been heavily involved with Super Hornet development and test work from the outset. Cdr Chubb, an ex-F-14 RIO continued, 'Current significant programs for the Super Hornet

Above: **Devil's playground – over the awesome backdrop of the Owens Valley stretching away to the north, a VX-31 F-model 'Rhino' pulls into a hard left-hand turn.** *Jamie Hunter/AVIACOM*

Above right: **High above the Sierras and looking back towards desert and Owens Dry Lake in the distance, an F/A-18F cruises above stunningly contrasting terrain.** *Jamie Hunter/AVIACOM*

include all software block upgrades, APG-79 AESA radar, Joint Helmet-Mounted Cueing System (JHMCS) for the rear seat of the F/A-18F (as well as the F/A-18D), EA-18G lead-in work and the Shared Reconnaissance Pod (SHARP). All weapons that are carried on the Super Hornet must complete developmental test at VX-31 prior to going to Operational Test (with VX-9)'. One significant new weapon that is planned for the Super Hornet is Lockheed Martin's Joint Common Missile (JCM). This has undergone warhead penetration tests to destroy urban targets and is being developed as the next-generation multi-purpose air-to-ground precision missile to replace Hellfire, Longbow, Maverick and airborne TOW missiles.

The development path for JCM has however been far from smooth with a number of proposed terminations.

The latest radar for the Super Hornet is the agile-beam Raytheon APG-79 AESA (Active Electronically Scanned Array), an integral element of the Navy's Block II upgrade for the jet. The APG-79 will supersede the APG-73 currently installed in new-build Super Hornets from 2007, and will also be available as a retrofit for existing examples. However, the redesigned forward fuselage required to accommodate the AESA radar means that Super Hornets built prior to Lot 26 would need to be structurally modified to accommodate the new radar. The program was in the Engineering and Manufacturing Development (EMD) stage in 2004 and operational evaluation is planned for spring 2006 with VX-9. The multi-mode APG-79 vastly improves target detection ranges to allow air-to-air missile launch at maximum range and it can almost simultaneously operate in air-to-ground modes, with incredible mapping and identification attributes. As well as testing the new radar with the AIM-120 AMRAAM, testing in 2005 for the AESA-equipped test F/A-18F included dropping a pair of 2,000 lb JDAMs, with the

bombs crossing in flight to reach targets on opposing sides of the aircraft, a first for the 'Rhino'.

The Shared Reconnaissance Pod (SHARP) system is designed to replace the F-14 Tomcat's TARPS (Tactical Air Reconnaissance Pod System) and was approved for Low Rate Initial Production in 2002, with a number of early pods deployed with VFA-14 and VFA-41 in time for Operation *Iraqi Freedom* (OIF). According to Cdr Chubb, 'The sensors are coming along, and so is the datalink. We fly it on F/A-18Es during testing but the plan is to deploy on the F-model only. The way it is mechanised means that it is a credible single-seat mission due to the ability to pre-plan missions and load them into the SHARP pod'.

Another significant program for the Super Hornet is the Raytheon ASQ-228 Advanced Targeting Forward-Looking Infra-Red (ATFLIR). VX-31 completed developmental testing on Block I capabilities prior to fleet release in 2002 and the Navy initially deployed pre-production pods, and received a batch of much-improved LRIP ATFLIR pods in time for OIF. The Super Hornet can also carry the original AAS-46 Nite Hawk pod which has been modified for use on the

Above: **Cdr Tim 'Eel' Morey noses his F/A-18E into tight formation, offering the opportunity to compare the E and F Super Hornet models.** *Jamie Hunter/AVIACOM*

Right: **Up close with Cdr Chubb in 'his' personalised F/A-18F.** *Jamie Hunter/AVIACOM*

Below right: **'Coso' in the climb.** *Jamie Hunter/AVIACOM*

Super Hornet. The ATFLIR pod gives the Super Hornet radically enhanced targeting capabilities and can be coupled up to the JHMCS and used in conjunction with the APG-79 to give an impressive all-round ground targeting and imaging capability. Raytheon has introduced a new high-speed datalink for ATFLIR, a capability at the heart of the Super Hornet's development as a critical node of the battlefield network, able to share data with offboard platforms and ground forces. ATFLIR's new Ku-band datalink offers a huge improvement in speed, with growth potential for full duplex (two-way communication) functionality along with a sophisticated encryption system to protect the flow of information. Capt Don Gaddis, US Navy F/A-18 program manager commented, 'Fast and secure communications are crucial in the highly mobile and dynamic battlefield of today and the future, to ensure the correct targets are engaged and the appropriate engagement decisions are made'.

Above: **Lt Col James 'Hawk' Hawkins at the controls of VX-31's TAV-8B Harrier. This aircraft has been heavily involved in developing flight controls for the new Joint Strike Fighter (JSF).** *Jamie Hunter/AVIACOM*

Bottom: **'Dust Devils' F/A-18E and TAV-8B break for action.** *Jamie Hunter/AVIACOM*

PROWLER TO GROWLER

As Cdr Chubb mentioned, VX-31 is already hard at work on lead-in studies for the US Navy's next-generation electronic attack aircraft – the EA-18G, unofficially dubbed the 'Growler'. This derivative of the F/A-18F with 90% commonality is slated to replace the EA-6B, with a plan for system integration testing at VX-31 already under development. The squadron has completed numerous aircrew workload evaluations during simulated missions for the platform, and is also developing a model for test teams to ensure that mission oriented development test (DT) and operational test (OT) will be as efficient and streamlined as possible. The 'Dust Devils' expect delivery of the first test EA-18G to China Lake in November 2006 with testing to begin shortly thereafter. Operational Evaluation (OPEVAL) is scheduled for August 2008 with IOC in September 2009. With the first EA-18 (EA1) expected to fly in 2006, the timeline to fleet deployment will undoubtedly result in a busy test period for VX-31. The Navy expects to purchase 90 EA-18Gs to completely replace the latest-standard ICAP-III EA-6B Prowler by 2012, equipping a single five-aircraft squadron for each of the ten air wings (CVWs), plus a training squadron. The aircraft will be adaptable and able to carry weapons loadouts to accomplish 'swing-role' missions with various stores permutations, including ALQ-99 jammer pods, AARGM, JSOW, AIM-120 AMRAAM and AIM-9X. As a particular campaign develops, the versatile EA-18G could theoretically turn its hand to more conventional missions as required to supplement other carrier strike assets.

Left: **Over the uniquely coloured Owens Dry Lake, Cdr Morey and Capt Chubb in Super Hornets move into close formation on the F/A-18F camership near China Lake.** *Jamie Hunter/AVIACOM*

Bottom left: **The Mojave desert's military operating areas (MOAs) offer year-round excellent flying conditions.** *Jamie Hunter/AVIACOM*

Right: **Armed with an AGM-154 JSOW, a VX-31 F/A-18F Super Hornet is loaded ready for a test mission with the weapon.** *Jamie Hunter/AVIACOM*

Left: **The JSOW-toting Super Hornet heads out from runway 21 at China Lake. The squadron has a huge diversity of ongoing programs and weapon systems that are being developed such as AARGM (AGM-88E Advanced Anti-Radiation Guided Missile), AGM-154 JSOW-C (Joint Stand-Off Weapon), JDAM (Joint Direct Attack Munition) with anti-GPS jamming enhancements and the Raytheon AIM-9X.** *Jamie Hunter/AVIACOM*

Below left: **With the heat shimmering off the runway, a VX-31 'Dust Devils' F/A-18F piles on the power as it leaps into the air from China Lake for an AIM-7 integration test mission. The Joint Helmet-Mounted Cueing System (JHMCS) was introduced for Super Hornet pilots as part of the Block I upgrade. VX-31 has also cleared the helmet for use in the rear cockpit.** *Jamie Hunter/AVIACOM*

Below: **Cdr Tim Morey assumed command of VX-31 in September 2005 and is seen here taxying in at China Lake toting a pair of test GBU-31 JDAMs on his F/A-18F.** *Jamie Hunter/AVIACOM*

Above: **Lt Cdr 'Doc' Shoemaker, flying this F/A-18F, was a project pilot at VX-31 for the APG-79 AESA radar program for the Super Hornet.** *Jamie Hunter/AVIACOM*

Left: **Both US Navy and Marine Corps test pilots fly with VX-31, and like the USAF the Navy is integrating development and operational testing to eliminate redundant testing, share resources, detect problems earlier and reduce the time required to get new systems into the fleet.** *Jamie Hunter/AVIACOM*

Below: **With the moon in the background, VX-31 F/A-18F Super Hornet callsign 'Coso 51' climbs over the Sierra Nevada. This photograph was taken near Sequoia National Park and Mount Whitney, at 14,494ft the highest point in the continental US.** *Jamie Hunter/AVIACOM*

Left: **VX-31's TAV-8B flown by Lt Col James 'Hawk' Hawkins cruises against a gin-clear Californian sky.** *Jamie Hunter/AVIACOM*

Below: **Cloud partially obscures Mount Whitney as 'Coso flight' cruises north towards Lone Pine, over some of the most stunning scenery in the USA.** *Jamie Hunter/AVIACOM*

Bottom: **This VX-31 F/A-18F Super Hornet is carrying the original NiteHawk targeting pod rather than the new ATFLIR. The ATFLIR pod gives the Super Hornet radically enhanced targeting capabilities and can be coupled up to the JHMCS and used in conjunction with the APG-79 radar to give an impressive all-round ground imaging capability.** *Jamie Hunter/AVIACOM*

INSIDE THE RHINO

The Super Hornet cockpit is dominated by four main multi-function displays (MFDs). The central Multi-Purpose Colour Display (MPCD), popularly used for the moving map, is flanked by a pair of traditional 'green' MFDs. The touch-sensitive up-front controller screen in the centre is supplemented by a wide-angle head-up display (HUD – in the front only in the two-seat F/A-18F). The Weapons System Officer (WSO) station in the rear seat of the F-model is being upgraded with the new advanced aft crew station with a large 8x10in advanced display as part of the Block II upgrade. The new rear cockpit features in Lot 26 F-models and above. Lot 27 aircraft will be delivered with the 8x10in display. Block II aircraft will also include the AESA radar, multi-functional information distribution system (MIDS) and ATFLIR.

Commander's Perspective

Promoted in late 2005, Capt Chubb moved to a new post at Patuxent River. As is usual practice, the Chief Test Pilot (CTP) assumed command, in this case the highly-experienced test pilot Cdr Timothy Morey: 'Quite simply, as the squadron Commanding Officer, I am responsible for everything here. Mission accomplishment, the protection of our human and material resources, the professional development of our assigned people, sound financial management to ensure we are good custodians of our nation's federal funds, enforcement of Navy regulations, and along with that, the maintenance of good order and discipline. At the end of the day, the bottom line is safe and efficient flight testing. Everything else is absolutely required to produce that service. In the early years, our predecessors were flying completely new aircraft rather routinely. Today, new aircraft come along much more infrequently. When they do come along, the fidelity of the data, in real time, and the effect that today's computing power has on the analysis of that data has had a tremendous impact on modelling and simulation. I do not think that modelling and simulation will ever completely replace flight testing, but its contribution to flight testing as compared to the early years can not be overlooked. I think we assume much less risk today then our pioneers did in the early years. They also lost a lot of great test pilots.

'Today's development programs are extremely complex and our aircraft and weapons systems are highly integrated, much more so than back in the 1950s and 1960s. Many test programs struggle to evaluate aircraft dependent upon millions of lines of software code; finding the right balance of simulation and flight testing, all while conducting these test programs faster and with less cost. Classic flight test techniques still apply for basic aircraft performance and flying qualities, and they were developed "in the early years". But testing complex systems in a highly integrated aircraft is a daunting task. We are integrating our DT and OT flight testing in order to eliminate redundant testing, share resources, detect problems earlier, and reduce the time required to get new systems into the fleet. Integrated DT/OT has affected our operations only to the extent that it has complicated our scheduling process and we are working to alter our existing processes.

'There is no doubt that UAVs are in our future. They continue to evolve, and there are many questions that still have to be answered in order to incorporate them fully into our battlespace. They are combat proven, and there is no question in my mind that we have just started to tap into their utility in combat operations. In terms of the most memorable flight tests, if you ask a test pilot a common theme among the answers will be tests that involved a large volume of challenges and obstacles along the way. For me, it was a rather obscure test program where we wanted to know if removing the existing internal fuel tank air pressure regulator as installed in the FA-18 would result in fuel bladder structural issues. An engineer approached me and told me that he needed to do 90° supersonic dives from 50,000ft. I said, "Cool, I'm your guy!". A couple of days later, as I started to refine exactly what was going to be required to get useful data, the engineer added the additional requirement to do these dives with almost no fuel in the tanks. This program involved testing unique fuel transfer procedures, instrumentation modifications, simulator development of the proper test technique, environmental approval because of the sonic booms, development of dive recovery tables because existing ones did not come close to 90°, and flight clearance issues involving the unique G environment in a pure 90° dive. It was fun, and in the end we reduced the weight of the aircraft, improved maintainability, and saved about $26m in production costs!'

On the flightline at VX-31, the F/A-18C Hornet fleet is receiving a number of new upgrades to address new and future fleet requirements. The type will eventually be replaced in service by the F-35C Joint Strike Fighter (JSF). *Jamie Hunter/AVIACOM*

A 'Dust Devils' F/A-18D Hornet leaps into the air at China Lake carrying a centreline Litening targeting pod. The Litening pod has proved extremely effective and the US Marine Corps is looking to expand this from the original centreline fit to the 'cheek' pylon on the D-variant Hornet. *Jamie Hunter/AVIACOM*

IMPROVING THE LEGACY

Cdr Rick 'Skyler' Botham is an experienced Naval Aviator, having flown the A-7E Corsair and F/A-18A to D Hornet since joining the Navy in 1984. He is heavily involved in 'Legacy' Hornet test flying at VX-31. 'This is my third tour here at China Lake. I converted to the A-7 with VA-174 before joining VA-37 "Bulls" before my first spell flying here at China Lake from 1990 with VX-5, flying the A-7 and then the A-4 Skyhawk. I converted to the Hornet in February 1991 and found myself back here in October 1997 with the "Dust Devils". After a tour on the USS *Harry S Truman* battle group staff I came back to VX-31 as XO. I fly A and B Category test on the F/A-18A, B, C and D, which usually means flying four to five times a week. We are busy working on the 19C OFP (Operational Flight Program) for the US Navy and USMC Hornet with Link-16 datalink, ATFLIR, JHMCS, the new tactical moving map (TAMMAC), electronic warfare upgrades and the new Joint Mission Planning System (JMPS). I hold a dual NATOPS qualification which means that I also fly the Metroliners on passenger and logistics flights to our sister station at Point Mugu.' Some of the most interesting missions being flown by Cdr Botham

are in the AESA Super Hornet target aircraft. VX-31 operates a handful of 'clean' F/A-18As to act as highly manoeuvrable targets to develop and test the new radar system. As with many development test and operational test units, VX-31 is increasingly combining testing with co-located VX-9 as Capt Chubb explained, 'The next two software upgrades for the Hornet family (19C and H2E+) are beginning Integrated Test and Evaluation (IT&E). The APG-79 program has enjoyed successful combined testing with VX-9, with this streamlined test process proving effective thus far, and has the potential of delivering products faster and cheaper to the fleet.'

The US Marine Corps' Hornets are the focus of some interesting programs at VX-31 as new capabilities are introduced to keep the type potent. Maj Danny 'Jerky' Johnson is a USMC Hornet pilot assigned to the unit: 'We are working a number of projects for the D-model. We have AIM-9X and JHMCS in the rear cockpit, but the Link-16 is a big thing for us working in the Close Air Support (CAS) role because we can get Nine Line Brief (NLB) target information and also imagery from the FAC (Forward Air Controller). The Navy has cancelled JASSM, but we are now testing JSOW with a new target of opportunity mode. We are also getting the dual mode guided bomb with GPS and laser guidance. The Litening pod has proved extremely effective and we are now looking to move this from the original centreline fit to the "cheek" pylon on the Hornet.'

Above: **This F/A-18C of VX-31 is seen fitted with Triple Ejector Racks (TERs) and orange test AIM-9 Sidewinder missile rails.** *Jamie Hunter/AVIACOM*

Left: **Wearing the JHMCS helmet, Cdr Rick Botham taxies in at China Lake in an F/A-18C.** *Jamie Hunter/AVIACOM*

Below left: **This VX-31 F/A-18A wears a desert splinter camouflage that has been retained from its time on the strength of NSAWC (Naval Strike Air Warfare Center) at NAS Fallon, NV. The aircraft is used primarily as a target aircraft for radar and captive missile trials.** *Jamie Hunter/AVIACOM*

Below: **With its two General Electric F414-GE-400 engines hissing, an AIM-7 Sparrow-armed 'Dust Devils' F/A-18F returns from a weapons testing mission.** *Jamie Hunter/AVIACOM*

Above: **'Devil formation'. A quartet of VX-31 aircraft form up above China Lake for a unique squadron photograph, led by Cdr Chubb in F/A-18F '201' with Cdr Morey in F/A-18E '200', Cdr Botham in F/A-18A '306' and Lt Col Hawkins in the TAV-8B.**
Jamie Hunter/AVIACOM

Left: **Cdr Tim Morey in his immaculate F/A-18E leads Lt Col 'Hawk' Hawkins in the TAV-8B Harrier. The 'Dust Devils' specialise in weapons capability developments for these two vital combat aircraft. The Super Hornet has stamped its mark on the US Navy fleet and offers a raft of capabilities.**
Jamie Hunter/AVIACOM

HARRIER TEST

The majority of testing for the US Marine Corps AV-8B Harrier II is conducted by the elite VX-31 and VX-9 pilots at China Lake working increasingly as a combined team. According to one VX-31 test pilot, 'Once a product has attained reasonable reliability and maturity, we invite OT (operational test) pilots to fly as well. This process allows for early recognition of possible issues so that they can be resolved prior to a product officially entering OPEVAL'. The AV-8B H2.0 OFP has recently been completed at China Lake, according to Maj James Coppersmith, and it is being introduced to the fleet. This fully integrates the Litening Pod as a sensor for the Harrier and allows ordnance to be employed against whatever the pod is tracking, as well as allowing pod-derived target co-ordinates to be seamlessly passed to JDAM. The pod's laser can now be used as a height-above-target source, which increases bombing accuracy and improves the quality of target co-ordinate generation. The Predator Video Downlink is a transmitter installed internally in the Litening Pod and allows for real-time streaming video to be sent to a Rover ground station. This capability greatly improves communication between Forward Air Controllers (FACs) and strike aircraft as well as greatly reducing the possibility of collateral damage and fratricide. The new upgrade also integrates the 500 lb GBU-38 JDAM – small urban precision bomb.

According to Maj Coppersmith, the next upgrade is the H4.0 for the Harrier. This involves increased warload with additional smart weapons carriage capability thanks to the digital improved triple ejector rack (ITER) to allow more than one GBU on each station. AV-8B Joint Systems Support Activity (JSSA) at China Lake, is a partnership between the USMC Harrier program and both the Italian and Spanish Harrier programs. Most of the things we test at China Lake are delivered to all three nations, however we sometimes conduct specific testing for a particular customer. A good example of this was the AIM-120B AMRAAM integration effort which was executed based on Spanish and Italian requirements.

Above: **Maj Bill Rothermel goes through lengthy cockpit checks prior to start-up in the upgraded AV-8B. This aircraft features H4.0 software that enables increased warload with additional smart weapons carriage capability thanks to the digital improved digital triple ejector rack (ITER).** *Jamie Hunter/AVIACOM*

Left: **The unmistakable shape of the APG-65 radar-equipped AV-8B+. The US Marines operate around a hundred of these potent Harriers.** *Jamie Hunter/AVIACOM*

Right: **VX-9 'Vampires' AV-8B+ Harrier taxies out.** *Jamie Hunter/AVIACOM*

Below: **'Break, break…go!'** *Jamie Hunter/AVIACOM*

On the Range

The China Lake range complexes are instrumented with precision radar and laser tracking systems supplemented by a network of high-powered cameras for still and video links back to base. The quality of the network allows analysts to follow aircraft from the ramp to the range, watch them expend live ordnance and then watch them (still on precision tracking cameras) all the way back to the runway! The Electronic Combat Range (ECR) located 30 miles south-east of the main base, permits analysis and development of systems that counter or penetrate air defences. Electronic warfare resources here are the primary assets available to the US Navy and include a full complement of actual and replicated sea and land based threats including SAM missiles, runways and hangars to add realism in support of electronic combat training, testing, tactical development and special operations. The command and control capabilities of the ECR Range are constantly updated to mirror the current World situation, those flying the range can expect an intelligent opponent with an awesome threat capability. Test scenarios can involve an aircraft being 'painted' by up to four acquisition radars during flight, then being handed off to appropriate target engagement sites. Aircrews and ECM suites have only a few seconds to counter the threats before simulated SAMs or anti-aircraft artillery (AAA) open up on them. With some of the Range's air defence traps, an incoming aircraft can be tracked by up to twelve engagement radars, making reaction time critical. With such qualities, the China Lake ranges attract a growing number of customers, with the test units at Edwards being a key user. The RAF is also a regular visitor, with the Fast Jet Weapons Operational Evaluation Unit (FJWOEU) conducting annual deployments. China Lake is an ideal location with the required resources for extended periods of live weapons and EW trials. The Advanced Weapons Laboratory here is a large hangar isolated in the middle of the Station housing the unique F/A-18 Hornet WSSA (pronounced 'Wisser'). This is the Weapon System Support Activity and serves to evaluate new mission suites for incorporation onto all Hornet variants. The hangar features an external 108-foot tall mast-like tower that accommodates the Hornet's mission sensors. The WSSA takes the form of an advanced simulator that is linked to laboratories and the China Lake/Point Mugu ranges. This means that as well as being able to interface 'real-time' with live weapons, Electronic Warfare scenarios, or an actual airborne aircraft, the WSSA can theoretically attack real or simulated targets in a bid to examine and refine the Hornet's mission as the spearhead of all potential front line operations.

Above left: **One of VX-31's Search and Rescue (SAR) HH-1Ns scoots between the canyons near China Lake on a training mission flown by Lt Kent Jones.** *Jamie Hunter/AVIACOM*

Above: **The squadron also operates this special T-39D Sabreliner that can be configured with different noses to carry test instrumentation for missile seeker head technology.** *Jamie Hunter/AVIACOM*

Left: **Desert treasure – one of the fascinating compounds of derelict airframes at China Lake. Of note here are a B-29 Superfortress, RA-5C Vigilante and one of the original F-111Bs built for the US Navy before the program was cancelled.** *Jamie Hunter/AVIACOM*

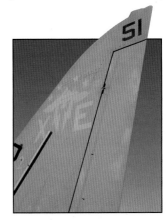

A VX-9 'Vampires' F/A-18D taxies out past the vintage squadron hangar at China Lake, this hangar dates back to World War Two.
Jamie Hunter/AVIACOM

VAMPIRE VALUES

Across the flightline at China Lake is Air Test and Evaluation Squadron Nine (VX-9) 'Vampires', and as mentioned previously this is the squadron responsible for operational test (OT) of new weapons systems for US Navy and Marine Corps strike aircraft. The squadron was formed out of the amalgamation of VX-4 'Evaluators' at Point Mugu and VX-5 'Vampires' at China Lake from 1993, with Hornet, Prowler, Harrier and AH-1 Cobra testing carried out at China Lake, and a permanent F-14 Tomcat detachment maintained at Point Mugu to cover the role previously undertaken by VX-4. The squadron's Point Mugu F-14 detachment sadly ended in 2004, with the China Lake activities now forming the focus for all of the unit's work.

The squadron's role encompasses realistic operational testing of fighter, attack and electronic warfare attack aircraft and developing tactical procedures for their employment. This results in a particularly hectic schedule for the squadron, with over 40 major projects likely to be running at any given time for the squadron fleet. Unlike VX-31, the aircrews here are mainly straight from the fleet – pilots with recent fleet experience to allow realistic operational evaluation of a new system. Results of a trial will be written up as a test report and a recommendation provided for the fleet.

The squadron will typically be involved in a new project right from the beginning, inputting early ideas into the workflow through Initial Operational Test and Evaluation (IOTE). As a program progresses through development test at VX-31, VX-9 will be gearing up for the formal Operational Evaluation (OPEVAL) phase. It makes for an extremely diverse and challenging mission.

Commanding VX-9 in 2005 was Capt Bruce Fecht: 'My role is to ensure the production of our Operational Test programs are running efficiently and effectively to get the best systems to the fleet in the least amount of time. It's also to ensure the sailors, marines and civilians are working in a positive and productive environment. We are testing numerous systems on various platforms in different locations on a routine basis. My role as Commander is to lead and co-ordinate all these various factions to ensure we are supporting the fleet in their operational efforts and I believe we are taking a much more dedicated business approach to flight testing now.

'A number of new challenges have been thrown up by our new mission planning system JMPS (Joint Mission Planning System). It has run into a number of software problems that have created some challenges and delays thereby slowing down our test on the finished product. It also had some fiscal restraints that made it difficult for us to send folks to the fleet locations and meetings to tidy up the problems we have discovered. Luckily with lots of dedicated folks putting in some extra time and brainpower we are arriving at a product we think we can send to the fleet with a certain level of confidence in its utility for aircrew. Eventually it will be a much better system than what we currently use so we are pushing hard to make this right and get it to the flight line. Even as I discuss this we have a couple of folks under way on a carrier in work-up to give it that real world test to ensure its viability under those stressful conditions.

A 'Vampire' Super Hornet pilot conducts a low-level pop-up manoeuvre over the Panamint Valley near China Lake. The aircraft was performing tests on the Shared Reconnaissance Pod system (SHARP) prior to fleet operational clearance. SHARP is a multi-function reconnaissance pod, adaptable to several airborne platforms for tactical airborne reconnaissance. *US Navy/Cdr Ian Anderson*

Right: Carrying an AIM-9X, VX-9's 'CAG' F/A-18E Super Hornet gets airborne from China Lake. The squadron conducts independent operational testing of weapons systems and develops tactics and procedures for mission employment for the Navy and Marine Corps. *Jamie Hunter/AVIACOM*

Below right: The famous 'Playboy Bunny' featured only briefly on VX-9 Super Hornets. After VX-9 pilots initially became qualified on the new Super Hornet at China Lake in 1999 the squadron took the aircraft through two weeks of day and night carrier operations aboard the USS *John C Stennis*. Here crews operated and supported the Super Hornets as an integrated part of the carrier's air wing (CVW). *Jamie Hunter/AVIACOM*

in the combat scenarios we required and the DT folks flying with us could then get a near real-time debrief of the issue and start working a solution immediately. It was nice to see a plan come together. My desire for the future is to shorten the timeline for test and ensure the priorities meet the fleet requirements before we direct assets towards any particular test. Along with that I want to ensure any new systems are consistent with our network-centric ideas for future combat and the exchange of data freely and effectively. Way down the road we are putting ideas together for future systems such as J-UCAS and JSF.'

Capt Fecht continued, 'I have lots of memorable test missions which have included dropping bombs, shooting missiles or just wringing out new systems so it's hard to pick just one. I have a certain good memory of an F-14 test I was involved in early in my tour at VX-9. The Tomcat was finishing up its last tape test for the final deployment in CAG-8 going on this very moment. It had to do with a Phoenix missile shoot and I was actually involved with launching the targets and "bustering" out of the way so the shooters could get a "green" (clear) range. It was fun scenario and the aircrew, range controllers, and all the systems worked just as planned. I was able to see a couple of those big Phoenix missiles light off for one last time and being a Tomcat pilot from way back it made my day to see the old war horse doing it so well to the very end. Like many other platforms over the years, the Tomcat is done with test and we move on to test the new improved systems. I'm really happy and proud to be part of such a unique unit and group of highly professional aviators and maintainers all coming together to keep the tip of the spear sharp as we can test it.'

It is regular practice for VX-9 to deploy with a carrier air wing (CVW) for its trials and interaction with frontline units is very much what the 'Vampires' mission is all about. Once the groundwork is

'We are seeing certain trade-offs in attempting to streamline the DT and OT test process. We have to get involved earlier in the process which requires time, money and people skills that we usually aren't assigning in that part of the test cycle. However, the pay-off is we get a better OT look at the systems and can discover problems or methods we would like to see changed much earlier than before. We believe this saves time and money in the long run since we can gain that synergy of effort a lot sooner. During our co-operative DT/OT air-to-air detachment for software tape 19C on the "Legacy" Hornet we saw the combined effort really made for a quick turnaround on many of the deficiencies we found. We could test it

complete, if the program is successful the staff at the squadron write reports, draw up tactics and write manuals for the fleet to use. However, if a project fails to satisfy the team it has the power to say 'no we don't recommend this for introduction, either don't buy it or refine it'. The unit conducts its missions as a regular fleet pilot would, enabling any problems to be realised, with most aircrews here being regular fleet aviators.

It is clear that China Lake and its infrastructure holds a very special role in bringing new technology to the US military. In September 2004, a proposal was forwarded to US Defense Secretary Donald Rumsfeld to merge the China Lake, Edwards and Point Mugu facilities into a Joint Aerospace Research, Development, Test and Evaluation (RDT&E) centre, however the BRAC findings underlined how important these facilities truly are.

Right: **Armitage Field – home of VX-9 and sister squadron VX-31 'Dust Devils'.**
Jamie Hunter/AVIACOM

Below: **Initial operational evaluation (OPEVAL) for the Boeing Super Hornet began in May 1999 and lasted for six months. VX-9 crews put the Super Hornet through a complex variety of tactical missions representing the operational arena, flying more than 700 sorties to determine if the fighter was operationally effective and suitable.**
Jamie Hunter/AVIACOM

Above: **'Vampire' Hornets on the flightline at China Lake between operational test missions.** *Jamie Hunter/AVIACOM*

Left **VX-9 conducts operational test and evaluation for both the Navy and Marine Corps and is manned by personnel from both services.** *Jamie Hunter/AVIACOM*

Below: **VX-9 armourers prepare to load AIM-7 Sparrow missiles onto an F/A-18E during testing. The squadron regularly deploys from China Lake to participate in realistic training exercises. The squadron first took the Super Hornet to Red Flag at Nellis in late 1999.** *Jamie Hunter/AVIACOM*

Top: **Low level in the 'Sierras', a VX-9 F/A-18C gets down low during testing.** *US Navy/Lt Whiteside*

Above: **A clean 'Vampires' D-model Hornet taxies out past the famous air traffic tower and hangar at 'The Lake'.**
Jamie Hunter/AVIACOM

Above left: **The 'Vampires' completed operational evaluation of the ICAP-III EA-6B Prowler in 2005. This included embarking the Prowler aboard the carrier to test its suitability to all types of operations. Here the ICAP-III test aircraft makes an arrested landing aboard aircraft carrier USS *Abraham Lincoln* (CVN-72).**
US Navy/Lewis Hunsaker

Left: **High above the Nellis range complex in Nevada, a VX-9 EA-6B Prowler moves in to receive fuel from a USAF KC-135R. VX-9 no longer has Prowlers on full time strength and borrows aircraft as required from operational squadrons.** *Richard Collens*

VAMPIRE HISTORY

Today's 'Vampires' have evolved from diverse beginnings and have contracted in size as the operational inventory has consolidated on a handful of key aircraft types. The unit at China Lake actually started out as Air Development Squadron Five (VX-5) 'Vampires' back in 1951 at NAS Moffett Field to develop and evaluate tactics and techniques for delivery of airborne special weapons with the Douglas Skyraider. The mission expanded to take on new types as this important work developed, with the unit moving to China Lake in July 1956 to take advantage of the unique range and instrumentation facilities available here even back then.

In 1993, the squadron was merged with sister fighter evaluation squadron, the famous VX-4 'Evaluators' from Point Mugu, CA, to form VX-9 'Vampires' as a single operational test and evaluation squadron. A permanent F-14 Detachment was maintained at Point Mugu to continue Tomcat operational testing. Sadly, with the

The famous black VX-4 F-4J 'Vandy 1' fires Zuni rockets.

Mick Roth

Tomcat nearing the end of operational service, the 'Mugu Det' was disbanded in 2004, leaving China Lake as the home of the 'Vampires'.

Former VX-9 Point Mugu F-14 Detachment commander Lt Cdr Steve Leslie explained a little more about the vital work that the squadron undertook for the F-14 community prior to disbanding: 'We conduct all operational testing for the Tomcat's air-to-ground mission as well as most of the air-to-air work. Initially we get issued a mission statement which will basically outline a new system, so we go and evaluate its usefulness for the fleet. We decide how the squadrons will use it, check it out in all weathers, does it suit deck operations, does salt spray have an adverse affect, is it easy to maintain, can we really mess it up, basically does it serve its purpose? The F-14 was originally designed to have an air-to-ground capability and as the jet assumed its fleet defence role the A-6 Intruder became the prime attack platform. As the A-6 disappeared the Tomcat was in danger of becoming a victim to the Hornet. To keep the Tomcat viable within the fleet its multi-role talents needed unearthing. Once initial trials were completed at Pax River, we interfaced with the Intruder and Hornet community and adapted their tactics to make the Tomcat potent in the multi-role capacity.'

Left: **VX-4 'Evaluators' flew all US Navy F-4 Phantom variants to test the type under operational conditions. Here, VX-4's black F-4J 'Vandy 1' and white F-4S 'Vandy 5' jets (complete with famous 'Playboy Bunny') fly in formation carrying Zuni rocket pods.** *Mick Roth*

Bottom: **How times have changed. Back in 1972, VX-5 was operating a host of types in various colour schemes. This A-4M Skyhawk was photographed at China Lake in 1972.** *Mick Roth*

Right: **A pristine VX-5 'Vampires' Grumman A-6E Intruder carries a load of 'slick' bombs.** *Mick Roth*

Below right: **Photographed in 1975, a VX-5 A-7C Corsair takes off from Point Mugu following a visit from home station at China Lake.** *Mick Roth*

Chapter Six
Point Mugu

Home of the 'Bloodhounds'

It's a crisp golden sun-kissed autumn morning in California's Ventura County. The surfers are out in force enjoying the breakers along the coast and the traffic queues heading into Los Angeles are as bad as ever. In the southeastern corner of the Oxnard Plain, where the sea and the Santa Monica Mountains meet, is one of the US Navy's most famous flight test stations. Naval Base Ventura County Point Mugu has long been associated with some of the more interesting aircraft in service with the Navy thanks to the diversity of the testing conducted here.

'Put missiles in enemy cockpits and strike weapons through their front doors' is the mission statement of VX-30 'Bloodhounds'. This test squadron, formally known as Air Test and Evaluation Squadron Three Zero, was actually established back in May 1995 as Naval Weapons Test Squadron Point Mugu under the Naval Air Warfare Center (NAWC) competency realignment. The squadron previously existed under a number of identities but has remained the principal test unit for Point Mugu's Naval Air Systems Command assets and part of the NAWC Weapons Division.

The embryonic stages of testing here date back to January 1945 when the Loon surface-to-surface missile was evaluated as a potential ship-to-shore weapon. By 1949 Point Mugu was a Naval Air Station and the home of the Naval Air Missile Test Center, with the first stand-off air to surface missile, the radio-guided Bullpup, put to the test here in 1958, followed by the now famous AIM-7

Working the FCLP (Field Carrier Landing Practice) pattern at Point Mugu, Cdr Rich Burr, who became commander of VX-30 'Bloodhounds' in 2006, slams on the power and climbs away in his F/A-18A Hornet following a 2v1 basic fighter manoeuvres (BFM) mission over the nearby Pacific ranges. *Jamie Hunter/AVIACOM*

Sparrow. The adjacent Pacific Missile Range was soon linked via flight corridors to the similar facilities at China Lake. The early 1990s saw Mugu again re-named the Pacific Missile Test Center (PMTC) – now boasting a wealth of historic military milestones, indeed mention any weapons system in Naval aviation service and you can bet that Point Mugu had some involvement along the line. The partnership of the F-14 Tomcat's AWG-9 radar and it's unique AIM-54 Phoenix missile was forged here and acceptance trials of the jet and its systems were concentrated at Point Mugu until fleet service began in 1973.

Point Mugu has traditionally hosted an incredible mix of missions and types, with the combination of VX-30 'Bloodhounds' assets and the largest sea test range in the world ensuring that the station remained one of the last bastions of Navy fast jet flying in southern California. Many pilots here hark back to 'The Salad Days' when they still called Miramar home – how times have changed. The 'Bloodhounds' support cutting-edge research, development, test, and evaluation (RDT&E) of a number of US naval combat systems and to fulfil this demanding role employs a uniquely varied fleet of

Left: **Cdr Rich Burr pre-flights the Hornet.** *Jamie Hunter/AVIACOM*

Below: **The colourful selection of 'Bloodhounds' Hornet tails on the flightline at Point Mugu in September 2005.** *Jamie Hunter/AVIACOM*

Above: **Cdr Burr climbs aboard for a test mission. VX-30's Hornets are kept busy supporting fleet work-up exercises in the nearby Pacific ranges.** *Jamie Hunter/AVIACOM*

Below: **The VX-30 Hornets came from a number of units, including this A-model that retains its colours from its time with VFC-12 at Oceana.** *Jamie Hunter/AVIACOM*

Above: **The 'Bloodhounds' retired their F-4 Phantoms and F-14 Tomcats in 2004, receiving early F/A-18A/B Hornets as replacements. Similar in appearance to the early 1990s electronic warfare training squadron VAQ-34 'Flashbacks', the VX-30 Hornets also wear a red star on the vertical fins.** *Jamie Hunter/AVIACOM*

aircraft. This tradition of VX-30 operating a mixed and diverse fleet was sadly dealt a huge blow in 2003 when it was decided that the squadron's last F-14 Tomcats and QF-4 Phantoms would be retired from service. The squadron had been heavily involved in most upgrades for the Tomcat fleet and was the last Navy unit with a dedicated Tomcat test team. Alongside the F-14s, the last-ever flying US Navy QF-4 Phantoms operated with VX-30 fulfilling a unique, and some would say irreplaceable role. Sadly, for both it was the end of the line. VX-30 swapped its charismatic Tomcats and Phantoms for A and B-model Hornets – it was time to move on.

'BLOODHOUNDS' TODAY

The Sea Test Range next to Point Mugu stretches from the Big Sur south to the Mexican Border and has the awesome undersea and overwater environments required for complete test and evaluation of naval warfare systems. The range is fully instrumented over its 36,000 square miles and provides an expansive environment to safely conduct air, surface, and subsurface weapon testing. It can host complex full battle group Fleet exercises involving aircraft, sur-

face ships, and submarines. It even has an FAA-approved low-level route up to the land impact ranges at China Lake for cruise missile testing. The VX-30 NP-3D Orions provide range clearance in support of all weapons testing and operational firings and provide the capability to track targets in support of various missions through use of an extensive suite of sophisticated telemetry, radar, and optical systems, in addition to providing support missions for the Fleet. NP-3Ds with Extended Area Test System (EATS) 'billboard' fairing can track cruise missiles and have logged over 4,000 flight-hours

Above: **The specially-painted VX-30 Commander's jet. In 2005 the 'Bloodhounds' skipper was Cdr Tom Bourbeau. The squadron doesn't conduct development work for the Hornet and concentrates on supporting test programs.** *Jamie Hunter/AVIACOM*

Left: **'Bloodhound flight clear to start.' Cdr Burr signals to the groundcrew that he is starting up.** *Jamie Hunter/AVIACOM*

Below: **Lt Cdr 'Razor' Shick returns to Point Mugu in one of the squadron's F/A-18As. These aircraft are configured to carry the Tiger infra-red measuring pod to support trials.** *Jamie Hunter/AVIACOM*

ranging from the Atlantic to the Pacific, from the Caribbean to the far reaches of the Indian Ocean supporting different programs.

Built in 1957, the squadron's DC-130A was returned to squadron duties with VX-30 in 2002, having been in storage or away on maintenance for some time. The DC-130 is also a war veteran, having been called into action for Operation *Iraqi Freedom* (OIF). Having been in deep maintenance in Edmonton, Canada, with L-3 SPAR Aerospace, the aircraft (Bloodhound 497) was quickly bought back to operational readiness. Bloodhounds' skipper in 2003 was Cdr Wade 'Torch' Knudson, who recruited assistance from the co-located Channel Island C-130 Air National Guard unit at Point Mugu in order to get the 'Herc' back from the frozen Canadian facility and ready it to deploy to Kuwait. Cdr Knudson trained up as a C-130 captain and deployed with his team to Ali al Salem AB ready for the start of OIF. On arrival, the DC-130 crew was abruptly acclimatised as the first night included a number of chemical weapons attack warnings. Once missions commenced, the DC-130 was employed launching its BQM-34 Firebee target drones near Baghdad. These then dropped radar-jamming chaff and, until they ran out of fuel, circled the city as decoys to draw anti-aircraft fire away from coalition strike aircraft. One of them achieved some notoriety as its para-

The VX-30 fighter flightline at Point Mugu. These ramps have been home to a diversity of Navy test and development aircraft over the years, now the F/A-18A. *Jamie Hunter/AVIACOM*

chute was seen by local Iraqi militia descending into a reed bed in the Tigris River in downtown Baghdad. Graphic TV pictures showed the Iraqis firing into the reeds as they believed the parachute to be from a downed airmen – however most are agreed that this was probably a Firebee chute.

Having switched from Tomcats and Phantoms to a fleet of 'Legacy' F/A-18A/B Hornets in 2004, the mission of VX-30 changed somewhat. Cdr Rich Burr, Chief Test Pilot (CTP) in 2005 explained, 'Following the retirement of the F-4s and F-14s NAVAIR decided that TACAIR (tactical aircraft) support was still required for the Sea Test Range. We fly safety photo chase for programs including the NASA Scramjet, we still fly Tomahawk missile chase missions and also fly target profiles for radars and AMRAAM testing for which we carry the ACE pod (AMRAAM Captive Evaluation). We are directly involved in supporting the fleet during work up programs such as JTFEX. For this we fly against ships as aggressors carrying electronic warfare (EW) pods as opposition forces. We are also providing operational support for Fleet Readiness Program (FRP) supporting Cat 3 adversaries such as the Kfirs and the adversary force at NAS Fallon.'

Recent testing of new equipment over the Pacific ranges has included the hypersonic X-43A tests and more recently the joint Boeing, Defense Advanced Research Projects Agency (DARPA) and the Navy hypersonic strike demonstrator HyFly. An F-15E launched HyFly during testing at Point Mugu in October 2005 and

Above left: **With a single drop tank carried on the starboard wing in an asymmetric fit, 'Bloodhound 102' climbs out from runway 21 at Point Mugu.** *Jamie Hunter/AVIACOM*

Left: **Cdr Rich Burr conducts Field Carrier Landing Practice (FCLPs) on the cross runway at Point Mugu. Now also known as Naval Base Ventura County, Mugu is also home to the Pacific Fleet E-2C Hawkeye squadrons.** *Jamie Hunter/AVIACOM*

Top: **High above the Channel Islands national park off the California coast, VX-30's DC-130A Hercules turns for home. As well as fulfilling drone launch duties, this Hercules is used to haul equipment out to the San Nicholas facility.**
Jamie Hunter/AVIACOM

Right: **Feel the noise – an immaculate 'Bloodhounds' NP-3D Orion taxies in from the washdown ramp after a mission over the Pacific ranges. The 'billboard' antenna on the fin is used to track cruise missile testing. The squadron's 'new' replacement P-3Cs will not feature this modification.** *Jamie Hunter/AVIACOM*

the solid rocket booster successfully ignited and accelerated HyFly to Mach 3. This test was the second of five HyFly flight tests that are scheduled until 2007 and will accelerate the vehicle to Mach 6. The objective of HyFly is to mature hypersonic missile concepts and will feature a configuration that is compatible with launch from surface ships and submarines as well as fighter aircraft.

Also in October 2005, the AESA radar-equipped Super Hornet was flexing its muscles when a pair of F/A-18Fs from China Lake were engaged in a live AMRAAM missile shoot against a target drone launched from the VX-30 DC-130. The program is developing the Super Hornet capabilities with the new radar and testing is ramping up towards firing from far greater ranges.

Left: **The colourful VX-30 DC-130A saw combat operations during Operation** *Iraqi Freedom.* *Jamie Hunter/AVIACOM*

Below left: **One of the VX-30 NP-3Ds retains the original white and gull grey finish, seen here departing from Point Mugu to patrol the Pacific ranges. This example, 'Bloodhound 341', will be the last of the squadron's three NP-3Ds to be retired in 2009 and replaced by three ex-fleet P-3Cs.** *Richard Collens*

Right: **Days gone by. A VX-30 NP-3D Orion frames the QF-4 Phantom flightline in the background at Mugu in 1997.** *Jamie Hunter/AVIACOM*

Below: **This VX-30 KC-130F Hercules is one of two Hercules that have been transferred from the US Marine Corps. These are taking on tanking, transport and drone launch duties. They will also receive the APS-115 radar from the P-3 to undertake range clearance control duties.** *Jamie Hunter/AVIACOM*

Above left: **VX-30 'Bloodhounds' retired its last QF-4S Phantoms in 2004 as the type was finally retired. The F-4 has had a long and distinguished history in the US Navy and its performance remained unmatched by many aircraft still in service.** *Jamie Hunter/AVIACOM*

Above: **With J79 engines in full reheat, a QF-4N blasts out of Point Mugu in 1998.** *Jamie Hunter/AVIACOM*

Left: **Every dog has its day – CUJO is the name on the base of the rudder of this immaculate VX-30 QF-4S out over the Pacific on a mission from Point Mugu in November 2003. The names on the rudders of the last of the VX-30 Phantoms were fittingly of dogs – a tradition started by maintainers as a way to provide each aircraft with a unique canine identity.** *Jamie Hunter/AVIACOM*

NAVY PHANTOM'S LAST STAND

Until 2004 Point Mugu was the only place in the world one could see active US Navy F-4 Phantoms. The Phantom flightline at Point Mugu could usually be counted on to offer three or four jets prepared for the day's flying – depending on the schedule. The QF-4s at VX-30 were lovingly maintained by civilian contractors Dyncorp, most of whose personnel had long careers in the military supporting F-4s of one type or another. The Phantoms with VX-30 were finally retired in September 2004 when the last aircraft left Mugu for either museums or to sadly be destroyed as targets on range com-

plexes. The aircraft remained in service as test and support platforms and were ex-fleet examples converted to QF-4 standard by the Navy. These stalwarts could be conventionally piloted by the small team of Naval F-4 aviators or flown via remote control as unmanned aerial targets, like the examples across at the USAF's 82nd ATRS. Just three Navy pilots remained qualified to fly the QF-4s as they went into retirement. Aside from a single remaining QF-4N, the QF-4S+ was king here at the end of operations, all of which were adorned with the stunning 'Bloodhounds' dog head markings on the fin as well as a unique nickname stencilled on the base of the rudder. These wore a three-tone overall grey scheme and looked for all the world as if they were still in front line service.

But these Phantoms were QF-4s and have all been converted to Full Scale Aerial Targets (FSAT), or 'drones' – meaning most were eventually shot down as realistic targets in live missile testing. These ex-Navy or Marine Corps F-4s were drawn from storage for Naval QF-4 conversion at the Naval Air Depot (NADEP) at Cherry Point, NC. Here the internal avionics fit was modified to incorporate the NOLO (No Onboard Live Operator) remote controls and, depending on the life expectancy of the jet, incorporated relevant amounts of specialist test equipment. When the decision was made to drawdown US Navy QF-4 operations in 2002, the NADEP at MCAS Cherry Point set about converting its last Phantoms for 'drone' use. On 3 March 2003, VX-30 Phantom test pilot Rich 'Mink' Bryant delivered the QF-4S to the 'Bloodhounds'.

The very fact that the Phantom remained in use with the Navy until 2004 was testament to its capabilities – the F-4 remained uniquely

suited to the manned missions it performed. Its 'drone' capability proved extremely useful for missile testing. The F-4S features enlarged leading-edge slats, which, when extended, increased the jet's combat turning capability by as much as 50% as well as improving handling at low speed. It was regarded by most as the ultimate Phantom.

The Full Scale Aerial Target (FSAT) role saw the Navy QF-4s operated in a 'NOLO' capacity from the remote San Nicholas Island, off the coast from Point Mugu, with the pilot 'flying' the QF-4 from the safety of a ground station. These flights comprised only a fraction

Top: **Glory days – a view across the 'Bloodhounds' flightline in 1998. The newer QF-4S in the foreground was starting to take over from the QF-4N as the primary Phantom test platform with the squadron. Mugu has always harboured rarer Naval types and boasted exciting flying and continues to do so today. The venerable A-3 Skywarriors and A-7 Corsairs soldiered on here with VAQ-34 'Flashbacks' until the unit moved to NAS Lemoore and upgraded to F/A-18s before disbanding. The last Navy Corsairs, the EA-7Ls (formerly with VAQ-34), were operated by the 'Bloodhounds' until November 1994.** *Jamie Hunter/AVIACOM*

Left: **Long-time 'Bloodhounds' Phantom pilot Lt Cdr Chip Shanle climbs aboard a QF-4S in 1998 for a test mission.**
Jamie Hunter/AVIACOM

A sharkmouthed QF-4N Phantom eases out to runway 03 at Point Mugu for a mission in 1998. Most QF-4 missions here were manned, with a small percentage flown from San Nicholas Island as unmanned NOLO flights for live missile shots against a realistic target. *Jamie Hunter/AVIACOM*

of the overall mission tally for the VX-30 'Rhinos', with the QF-4s being relied upon heavily for missions ranging from simulating offensive anti-shipping missiles to high-speed weapons testing. The Phantoms regularly supported surface vessels for training exercises and to enhance threat awareness the Phantoms can employ the MA-31 high-speed aerial target based on the Kh-31 Russian anti-radar and anti-ship missile. The chasing of Tomahawk cruise missiles during testing was ranked by many pilots as the most exciting of the manned QF-4 missions. Once the Tomahawk was launched from the ship, the VX-30 pilots chased after it in the QF-4. This mission has now been taken on by the F/A-18s.

The decision to retire the QF-4s from the squadron and US Navy inventory marked the final end of US Navy service after some 44 glorious years. Cdr Knudson reflected, 'The F-4 has had a long and distinguished history in the US Navy. Every time I am fortunate enough to take one airborne I think about those that have gone before me and the advancements in technology that have kept Naval Aviation's capabilities on the cutting edge. It's interesting that the performance of the F-4, though serving primarily as a drone/target aircraft, is still unmatched by many aircraft still in service around the world'.

The first Navy Phantom 'drones' were QF-4Bs converted in the early 1970s for test operations at China Lake taking over from target drone QF-86 Sabres. The QF-4B was primitive, unable to pull

high-G and limited in pitch and roll. These were soon superseded by the more manoeuvrable QF-4N from 1983, entering service at Point Mugu from 1986. In the late 1990s, the QF-4S joined the ranks at VX-30. The Navy's QF-4s were originally to have been produced alongside the Air Force examples by BAE Systems Flight Systems (Tracor Flight Systems) at Mojave, but differences in inter-service priorities eventually led to separate programs. The ultimate QF-4S+ incorporates a new Electronic Warfare (EW) suite and Trimble GPS (Global Positioning System).

As for a replacement for these Phantoms, the USAF QF-4s at Tyndall AFB are now solely responsible for the Full Scale Aerial Target mission. Nothing else looks or sounds like a Phantom. With its 12° dihedral 'cranked' outer wings and huge intakes it looks like it means business. These final Phantoms continued to earn their keep for a long time, doing battle against the latest cutting-edge missiles, and sometimes still coming out on top. The few Naval Aviators that still called the Phantom 'their mount' were justifiably proud. Sadly this was a battle that even the mighty Phantom could not win.

NAVAL WEAPONS TEST SQUADRON
POINT MUGU

Above: **One of the last ever Navy F-4 aviators, Cdr Wade 'Torch' Knudson was the commander of VX-30 in late 2003 when this photograph was taken.**
Jamie Hunter/AVIACOM

Top left: **As the US Navy progressed to the QF-4S the traditional Day-Glo nose and tail markings started to disappear. This example was one of the last to sport these bright markings.**
Jamie Hunter/AVIACOM

Bottom left: **Last of the line, Cdr Wade Knudson at the controls of a VX-30 QF-4S in late 2003 over Channel Islands national park off the California coast.**
Jamie Hunter/AVIACOM

Left: **Groundcrews tend to 'The Ghost' – an immaculate white YF-4J used by the 'Bloodhounds' as an ejector seat test platform. This aircraft is now stored.**
Jamie Hunter/AVIACOM

Above: **Cdr Knudson noses in alongside the VX-30 DC-130A Hercules during a mission over the Pacific in 2003.** *Jamie Hunter/AVIACOM*

Left: **Roll with it! Photographed from the F-14D cameraship, Cdr Wade 'Torch' Knudson rolls the QF-4S in dramatic style. The aim of the original F-4S modification program was to extend the service life and enhance the F-4J variant. The F-4S was a highly capable dogfighter thanks to its enlarged leading-edge slats, which, when extended, increased the jet's combat turning capability by as much as 50 percent as well as improving handling at low speed.** *Jamie Hunter/AVIACOM*

Top right: **The characteristic smokey trails from the engines were not a feature of the F-4S, which was fitted with J79-GE-10B engines with low-smoke combuster and low-energy ignition.** *Richard Collens*

Right: **The irreplaceable F-4 Phantom, 'Bloodhound 126' breaks for the camera.** *Jamie Hunter/AVIACOM*

Above left: **Phantom in its element, Cdr Wade Knudson pulls the QF-4S into a 45° climb as he heads back to Point Mugu.** *Jamie Hunter/AVIACOM*

Left inset: **Over the deep blue of the Pacific – 'Bloodhound 126' turns for home. This QF-4S served with VFA-154 'Black Knights' during its operational Navy career.** *Jamie Hunter/AVIACOM*

Top: **With the California coast and Ventura in the background, QF-4S Phantom 'Bloodhound 126' positions for the break at Point Mugu.** *Jamie Hunter/AVIACOM*

Above: **A sight that is sadly missed – QF-4S 'Bloodhound 122' nicknamed 'SPUDS' comes in over the runway 21 threshold at Point Mugu under the expert control of Cdr Wade Knudson.** *Jamie Hunter/AVIACOM*

Right: **With drag chute trailing, a 'Bloodhounds' QF-4S taxies back to its parking slot at Point Mugu.** *Richard Collens*

LAST TOMCAT TESTERS

Left: **A unique shot of VX-30 QF-4S and F-14D in formation, taken from the VX-30 DC-130A over the Pacific in November 2003.** *Richard Collens*

Below left: **F-14D 'Bloodhound 200' was VX-30's last-ever Tomcat, it was also the last-ever example attached to a test squadron and was retired in August 2004. Seen here in happier days on the flightline at Point Mugu being prepared for a test mission.** *Jamie Hunter/AVIACOM*

Right: **Commanding VX-30 in 2005 was Cdr Tom Bourbeau, an experienced F-14 radar intercept officer (RIO). Seen here about to climb into an F-14B of the squadron in 2003 when he was Chief Test Pilot.** *Richard Collens*

Below: **The morning air is pierced by the unmistakable high-pitched whine of two General Electric F110 engines as a VX-30 F-14D Tomcat taxies out for an early morning test mission.** *Jamie Hunter/AVIACOM*

Below: **A Block IV Tomahawk cruise missile is escorted by a VX-30 F-14D Tomcat during a controlled test over the NAVAIR western test range complex. During the second test flight of this variant of missile it completed a vertical underwater launch and flew a fully- guided 780-mile course before impacting a designated target as planned.** *US Navy*

Above: **F-14D 'Bloodhound 200' flown by Lt Cdr Mark 'Friday' Thomas cruises off the California coast in November 2003 with the author in the back seat.** *Jamie Hunter/AVIACOM*

Above inset: **A sight that will be forever etched in the minds of those who have served and visited Point Mugu – a VX-30 F-14B Tomcat returns from a mission in late 2003. The Tomcat will be retired completely from the Navy inventory in 2006 when the last squadrons VF-31 'Tomcatters' and VF-213 'Black Lions' convert to the Super Hornet.** *Jamie Hunter/AVIACOM*

Right: **Pulling round into the traffic pattern at Point Mugu, a VX-30 QF-4S. With the mighty Phantom now retired by the US Navy, the USAF remains the only operator of the type in the US. It is a type that has provided sterling service for test units throughout its illustrious career.** *Jamie Hunter/AVIACOM*

Below right: **A memorable moment, following a photo mission in November 2003 the author joins Cdr Wade 'Torch' Knudson (left) and the other members of the flight for a unique photo opportunity in front of VX-30 QF-4S and F-14D.** *Richard Collens*

Last Tomcat Testers

During Operation *Iraqi Freedom* (OIF) in 2003, VX-30 test teams cleared the F-14D to carry the GBU-31 Joint Direct Attack Munition (JDAM), before heading out to the aircraft carriers in the Persian Gulf to ensure that capability was bought to the fleet in time for combat operations. Other significant programs in 2003 included the release of three major Operational Flight Programs (OFPs) for the F-14D, integrating GPS navigation, APG-71 radar high resolution mapping, GBU-24 laser-guided bomb integration, improved and updated Airborne Self Protection Jammer, ALR-67 radar warning receiver and the Infra-red Search and Track (IRST) system.

In September 2004 F-14D 'Bloodhound 200' got airborne from Point Mugu for the last time and headed for the boneyard at Davis-Monthan AFB, AZ. The final departure had been slightly delayed to get the latest software (D05) cleared for the fleet. The replacement Hornets had a lot to live up to as new skipper Cdr Tom Bourbeau reflected, 'I'll personally miss the Tomcat's high speed, high endurance, and long-range capabilities. Also, the ability to find and engage aerial targets at much longer ranges than other current fighters. And most importantly, the Tomcat always attracted the best-looking women at airshows – annoying our Air Force F-15 and F-16 brethren!' For the 'Bloodhounds' filling the F-4 and F-14's large and highly capable shoes was not easy and the squadron was clearly sad to see them both go.

The future for the 'Bloodhounds' will undoubtedly involve further change, and there are moves afoot that could see the squadron further amalgamated with the China Lake units as happened with VX-9.

The NP-3Ds will be retired by the end of the decade due to fatigue issues and three ex-fleet P-3Cs are expected here by 2010. The squadron will also retire the DC-130 in June 2006, instead operating two ex-US Marine Corps KC-130s ('Bloodhound 400/401'), both of which will be configured with the APS-115 radar for range co-ordination as well as being equipped with interchangeable pylons for the drone launch and tanker support missions.

Whatever the future holds for the 'Bloodhounds' it is clear that the mission they fulfil is as important as ever and they will adapt to face the future challenges, as do all of these remarkable test squadrons.

We hope you enjoyed this book . . .

Midland Publishing offers an extensive range of outstanding aviation titles, of which a small selection are shown here.

We always welcome ideas from authors or readers for books they would like to see published.

In addition, our associate, Midland Counties Publications, offers an exceptionally wide range of aviation, military, naval and transport books and videos for sale by mail-order worldwide.

For a copy of the appropriate catalogue, or to order further copies of this book, and any other Midland Publishing titles, please write, telephone, fax or e-mail to:

Midland Counties Publications
4 Watling Drive, Hinckley,
Leics, LE10 3EY, England
Tel: (+44) 01455 254 450
Fax: (+44) 01455 233 737
E-mail: midlandbooks@compuserve.com
www.midlandcountiessuperstore.com

US distribution by Specialty Press –
see page 2.

Aerofax
LOCKHEED'S SR-71 'BLACKBIRD' FAMILY

James Goodall and Jay Miller

Though only 50 of these craft were built, everything about them was unique. The stories of the development program, the General Dynamics 'Kingfish' competition, the M-21 and D-21 effort, the F-12 saga, and the operational history of the A-12 and SR-71 under the auspices of the CIA and the USAF are all covered in detail. The high-speed, high-altitude recce overflights performed by SR-71As from bases in the US, Japan and the UK during the Cold War are also covered.

Softback, 280 x 215 mm, 128 pages, 205 b/w, 43 colour photos, plus illusts
1 85780 138 5 **£15.99**

Aerofax
BELL BOEING V-22 OSPREY
Multi-Service Tiltrotor

Bill Norton

This technologically challenging tiltrotor project established in 1982. A transport aircraft style fuselage, able to carry 24 troops, is topped by a wing with two swivelling pods housing Rolls-Royce engines, each driving three-bladed prop-rotors. The USAF should receive the CV-22B for special missions, the US Marines the MV-22B assault transports and the Navy the HV-22B CSAR/fleet logistics version, but the program suffered setbacks, with initial operating capability now set for 2005.

Softback, 280 x 215 mm, 128 pages
174 colour, 60 b/w photos, 33 dwgs
1 85780 165 2 **£16.99**

Aerofax
LOCKHEED MARTIN F/A-22 RAPTOR

Jay Miller

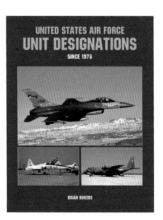

Initially referred to as the Advanced Tactical Fighter (ATF) the F-22 was designed to to replace the F-15 Eagle. In 1993 an air-to-ground attack role using precision-guided munitions was added to the air superiority role.

Now entering service at the end of a lengthy development program, the F-22 is designed to supercruise at up to Mach 1.5 without use of the afterburner and its unusual layout is designed for agility as well as to incorporate stealth characteristics.

Softback, 280 x 215 mm, 128 pages
282 colour, 48 b/w photos, 29 dwgs
1 85780 158 X **£16.99**

SEA HARRIER
The Last All-British Fighter

Jamie Hunter

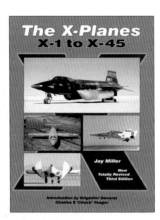

The Sea Harrier had proven its worth in combat over the Falklands within three years of entering frontline service. A Cold War warrior, and a veteran of recent actions in the Balkans, the Persian Gulf and Sierra Leone, the 'Shar' now finds itself at the end of its career. As well as extensive archive material and images from Sea Harrier pilots, the volume is illustrated with recent air-to-air and ground material taken by the author during the last two years of Sea Harrier operations.

Sbk, 280 x 215 mm, 160 pages
241 colour, 50 b/w photos, plus dwgs
1 85780 207 1 **£17.99**

THE X-PLANES
X-1 to X-45 (Third edition)

Jay Miller

This revised and updated version of 'The X-Planes' contains a detailed and authoritative account of every single X-designated aircraft. There is considerable new, and newly-declassified information on all X-Planes.

Each aircraft is described fully with coverage of history, specifications, propulsion systems and disposition. Included are rare cockpit illustrations. Each X-Plane is also illustrated by a detailed multi-view drawing.

Hbk, 280 x 216mm, 440pp, c980 photos including colour, c250 drawings
1 85780 109 1 **£39.95**

UNITED STATES AIR FORCE DESIGNATIONS SINCE 1978

Brian Rogers

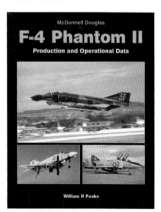

Designed to help identify the units to which Air Force aircraft have been assigned, this book has three major sections. First are 14 'chapters' containing tables covering every USAF wing, group, squadron, and detachment that was active and had assigned aircraft at any time between 30th April 1978 and 1st October 2002. Second is an index of aircraft markings, and then a chronology of major events in this reorganisation.

Softback, 280 x 215 mm, 272 pages, 32 pages of colour photographs
1 85780 197 0 **£24.99**

McDONNELL DOUGLAS F-4 PHANTOM II
Production and Operational Data

William R Peake

The McDonnell Douglas F-4 Phantom II is an aircraft with a long history and global presence. Although the F-4 is no longer in production, the 5,000+ airplanes have yet to be accurately chronicled on an individual basis.

The book lists each airplane in production order, and list block number, serial number, attrition date and circumstances, aerial 'kills', retirement date and circumstances, tail codes, and other essential details.

Softback, 280 x 215 mm, 360 pages, 191 colour photographs
1 85780 190 3 **£27.99**